Creativity: Revealing the Truth about Human Nature

First Edition Design Publishing

Creativity: Revealing the Truth about Human Nature

ISBN 978-1622-875-15-3 PRINT
ISBN 978-1622-875-16-0 EBOOK

LCCN 2014931741

January 2014

Published and Distributed by
First Edition Design Publishing, Inc.
P.O. Box 20217, Sarasota, FL 34276-3217
www.firsteditiondesignpublishing.com

"Each of us has a piece of the puzzle of solving the great world problems of our time and creating a more just, humane, and beautiful world. … If everyone who loved to create beauty did so, we would live in a beautiful world. If everyone who loved cleanliness and order, cleaned up, we would live in a clean and orderly world. If everyone who yearned to heal the sick did so, we would live in a healthier world. If everyone who cared about world hunger shared his creative ideas and acted to alleviate the problem, people would all be fed."

Carol Pearson

To

My Children
Dreams Come True

To

Dr. Richard J. Spady
World Futurist; Visionary; and Philanthropist

Creativity: Revealing the Truth about Human Nature

by
Efiong Etuk, Ph.D.

Table of Contents

Preface

"It is highly important, indeed urgently so, that we consider the possibility that our traditional ideas concerning the innate nature of man may be wrong and damaging, for I am convinced that underlying much of man's malfunctioning ... is this unsound conception of human nature."

--Ashley Montagu

This is the best of times. Ironically, it is the worst of times, also. Cursory review of the state of the world indicates a mixed blessing. On the positive side are: the highest standard of living the world has ever known; record production and consumption of goods and services; eradication of hitherto incurable diseases; unprecedented levels of physical comfort and material well-being; healthier lives and longer life spans; instantaneous communication across the globe; and a very long list of scientific and technological breakthroughs. Negative conditions include widespread poverty; hunger; misery; insecurity; fear; despair; prejudice; mutual distrust; destructiveness; group violence; ecological disasters; and, of course, the ever-looming threat of mutually assured destruction.

The questions arise:

> How could the most advanced civilization in human history give rise to so many crises: social crisis; economic crisis; financial crisis; humanitarian crisis; political crisis; energy crisis; raw material crisis; environmental crisis; and others?
>
> How could the highest standard of living the world has ever known leave practically everyone scared and, in many cases, fearing the worst?
>
> Why is it that the better things are, the unhappier people are becoming?

> Why is the world's dreadful situation continuing to deteriorate, despite all the time, effort, and resources that have been committed to its improvement?
>
> Are the modern crises unsolved because they are too difficult to solve, or because we have not yet found appropriate framework for understanding and resolving the seemingly separate problems?

The answer to these anomalies is the reason for this compendium of wit and wisdom on human nature.

While researching my earlier books on creativity, I came across several eye-popping representations of human nature that contradicted everything I had learned, or thought, about myself and other people. For years, I conveniently overlooked these seeming anomalies, and went on with whatever I was reading. But the contradictions kept recurring. One after another, they seemed to challenge the way humanity perceives itself. Eventually, I was persuaded; and I started to compile and reference these notions. The result is this compendium – a treasury of wit and wisdom bringing us face-to-face with our innermost nature.

Revealing, sobering, and at times convicting, the 1,771 insights that are brought together in this compendium represent perspectives from psychology, education, biology, medicine, sociology, business, political science, metaphysics, and the humanities. They are culled from the writings of some of the deepest thinkers, past and contemporary. The very large number of perspectives notwithstanding, every insight corroborates and complements the others.

The compendium is arranged alphabetically and numbered. Alphabetical arrangement makes it possible to read the book from practically any page, to the same effect. Numbering makes it easy to identify, highlight, and locate particular insights that speak to the reader deeply and personally. In order to maintain the integrity of the entries, insights are reproduced verbatim from their original sources and are fully and meticulously referenced, giving appropriate credit to their authors and sources.

Preliminary analysis of the compendium reveals a fundamentally new and authentic paradigm for thinking about ourselves. *Homo Creativus,* my term for the new understanding of human nature, signifies our quintessentially creative quality as humans. This is the fact that human beings are driven primarily to develop and to engage their unique abilities in significant, meaningful, and beneficial actions (with economic consumption and material well-being as the means to that end). Closer review of the insights yields three broad conclusions:

First, the generally accepted beliefs that people are inherently self-interested, competitive, adversarial, materialistic, and consumption-driven are both inadequate and misleading.

Second, most of the difficulties the world is experiencing seem to be rooted in the mistaken beliefs we hold about ourselves and the institutional framework and operational relationships we have erected on those beliefs.

Third, the best hope of resolving the modern crises is, first, to correct the inadequate and misleading beliefs we hold about ourselves and, second, to conform our economic, social, and political decisions and actions to our true nature.

This compendium, *Revealing the Truth about Human Nature,* offers the logical and necessary starting-point for the urgently needed correction. Sequel publications (in writing) entitled *Mass Creativity: A Global Imperative* provide the concepts and the application tools for translating the authentic concept of human nature into everyday activities.

My aim in compiling *Revealing the Truth about Human Nature* is primarily to call world attention to our essentially creative nature as humans. I particularly want to encourage readers to see themselves in new and authentic ways and, equally important, to become aware of misleading self-perceptions that have prevented the vast majority of people from reaching their full potential. The goal, ultimately, is to nurture a global creativity-consciousness – an approach to life and living in which human fulfillment and actualization of human potential are the guiding principles of society.

Revealing the Truth about Human Nature speaks to all people with a clear and pointed message that touches something basic in human nature and critical to our individual and collective well-being. Whatever their position or role in life, everyone will find this compendium an accessible and constant reminder of what we essentially are but, sadly, lost or allowed to atrophy. The veracity and universal applicability of the insights make the compendium a critical resource not only for personal effectiveness but also for professional relevance and success. The profundity of the insights is likely going to challenge and intrigue social scientists, social philosophers, business and political decision-makers for some time to come.

Revealing the Truth about Human Nature will be of particular interest to those social movements that are concerned with the dreadful situation the world is facing and that are working to save the Planet for future generations. The more widely reported of these are deep ecologists, peace advocates, women's movements, holistic health movements, human-potential movements, human rights advocates, ethnic liberation movements, and the large array of spiritual movements. People with responsibility for the growth and development of others will find *Revealing the Truth about Human Nature* a treasury of ideas for personal effectiveness and professional success. They include: helping professionals; educators; business and political leaders; human development professionals; public administrators; parents; care-givers; and international development professionals.

My hope is that the 1,771 insights that are brought together in this compendium and the authentic new understanding of human nature they have uncovered will significantly inform and facilitate the construction of potential-actualizing and humanly fulfilling institutions, organizations and, ultimately, global society. And I am confident that the universally accessible and pleasant-to-read format of the work will encourage and facilitate the largest possible public participation in the social reconstruction effort.

Efiong Etuk, Ph.D.

Acknowledgments

The great Michel de Montaigne characterized one of his many seminal works as a collection of other men's flowers for which he merely provided the thread. That's exactly how I feel about *Creativity: Revealing the Truth about Human Nature.* The 1,771 insights on human nature that are brought together in this compendium are, *all,* other people's ideas. I am deeply indebted to the authors of those gems of wisdom and, also, to the publishing houses that have preserved them for posterity.

I also wish to acknowledge the financial and intellectual support of two great visionaries: Dr. Richard Spady (President, Forum Foundation, Seattle, USA) and August Jaccaci (President, Unity Scholars, Thetford Center, Vermont, USA).

Members of the Blacksburg Church of Christ have been very generous and supportive for much of the time that I have been working on this book. Quite a great family!

I particularly wish to express gratitude to my wife, children, and brothers for their patient understanding. My children deserve eternal gratitude for their invaluable assistance in checking and cross-checking the accuracy of the materials that are the basis of this work.

Even with all the assistance that I have received in this work, several imperfections still remain for which I am solely responsible.

Foreword

Following in the footsteps of Erasmus' Adages and Bartlett's Familiar Quotations, Efiong Etuk has broken new and far more important ground. At a time when the first faint images of human extinction are emerging in the mirror of planetary nature, Etuk has supplied humanity with a compendium of profound insights on our potential creativity which literally redefines us all as architects of our own salvation on Earth. Never has the proof of human creative capability been more generously displayed.

August Thayer Jaccaci, Jr.
President, Unity Scholars, Thetford Center, Vermont, USA
Lifetime Achievement Award, Creative Education Foundation

Prologue

"Every engineer, every scientist, every farmer, and every mechanic knows that nothing will work, that no act will succeed, unless it is in harmony with ... the true nature of things as they are."

Henry Grady Weaver

Deep in the heart of every human being is the desire for his or her life to matter – the desire to bring about something new, unique, significant, and beneficial to others and the Planet. Where it is not artificially constrained, this desire has been observed across cultures and in practically every sphere of human activity. Anecdotal evidence and the wisdom of the ages show it to be the supreme goal of life, and its fulfillment as key to genuine and enduring success. Universal and intuitive, everyone experiences its reality almost all the time, even if we are not always consciously aware: The impulse for creativity and service that "clamors" for expression, and that will not stop its clamor until it is fulfilled.

When we are able to find a task that we are naturally good at or that we are uniquely equipped to perform, we experience inner joy and a sense of fulfillment, regardless of any frustrations, inconveniences, drudgery, pain, or loss. The feeling is the same when we find a local or planetary project that connects us to a larger purpose and that therefore gives meaning and significance to our life; when we find a goal that brings harmony to our existence; or when we are able to live up to our individual potential for excellence, service, and creativity.

However, when our daily life experience provides neither joy nor fulfillment, we tend to become unhappy, bored, depressed, or apathetic. In extreme cases, we tend to view our life as futile or meaningless. We might be able to surround ourselves with the finest things of the marketplace, and yet not be satisfied. The letters and designations after our name might signify academic or professional success when, deep within us, things are not quite right. The circumstances of our birth might bestow glamour and fame that we really don't care about or would rather do without.

These are not conjectures; they are tragic facts of modern life and living. Empirical and anecdotal evidence indicates widespread "personality disorders," with incalculable harm to families, communities, and workplaces. Consider, for example:

> "Busy-yet-bored employees whose hearts are not in the work they are doing."
>
> "Outwardly successful, yet emotionally troubled executives … honored and well-educated but without ever having experienced what it means to be truly alive."
>
> Many people who have all they've ever wanted but, self-reportedly, still feel "empty inside" and still look for something they say is missing from their lives.
>
> The prevalence of stress, depression, burnout, and emotional breakdown; consequently, the growing popularity of anti-depressants and various psycho-therapeutic procedures that purportedly "restore balance" in their users' lives.
>
> Prisons around the world that are "overflowing with inmates," and mental hospitals with "cases."
>
> "Hundreds of troubled young people who have so much to live for [but decide to] take their own lives every year."
>
> "Ever more people today [who] have the means to live but not the meaning to live for."
>
> "Most of us [who] go to our graves with our music still inside [unplayed, unheard]."

Conventional wisdom regards these tragic conditions as individual problems and, matter-of-factly, attributes them to personal inadequacies or the so-called "human propensity to evil." Based on assumptions of personal inadequacies, several person-centered solutions and remedies have been proposed and tried: counseling, therapy, motivation, reward, surveillance, deterrence, incarceration, punishment, rehabilitation, etc. The limited success of these interventions calls into question the assumptions of personal failings that inform them.

This compendium of insights on human nature poignantly demonstrates the inherent goodness of people and, by implication, challenges assumptions of innate human depravity. Short, simple phrases with life-changing meanings, the 1,771 gems of wit and wisdom that are brought together in this volume represent perspectives from psychology, education, biology, medicine, sociology, business, political science, metaphysics, and the humanities.

Analysis of the insights reveals our quintessentially creative, but historically overlooked nature as humans. *Homo Creativus,* my term for this image of man, signifies this essence. *Homo Creativus* represents man as a potential-actualizing being, driven primarily to develop and to engage one's particular set of abilities in meaningful, significant, and beneficial actions – with economic consumption and material well-being as the means to that end. (This is in contradistinction to the generally accepted conception of human nature as self-interested, competitive, adversarial, materialistic, and consumption-driven upon which most modern policies and decisions are based.)

From the compendium also emerge two broad conclusions with far-reaching implications for the way we perceive ourselves, organize society, and conduct affairs: First, the desire for meaning and fulfillment is the primary and most powerful motivating force in human life – the one need that drives all, or most, other needs. Second, the prevailing understanding of human nature as individualistic, self-centered, competitive, materialistic, and consumption-driven is not only incomplete, but at variance with the truth. By focusing largely on the material aspect of life, we seem to have overlooked what is most important in human life: Creativity, actualization of one's innate capacity for excellence and service, and the resultant sense of fulfillment that people's life and work should provide. One result of that deprivation is the spreading "epidemic" of meaninglessness, of which many psychological, social, and economic problems are the symptoms, or facets.

If, therefore, we are to be able to resolve many of the crises the world is experiencing, what is needed, first and foremost, is to correct the prevailing but misleading conception of human nature which, from all indications, is at the root of our present predicament. *Revealing the Truth about Human Nature* – this compendium of insights on human nature – presents a logical and necessary starting-point for that urgently needed correction.

***

Serendipity is a curious but apt description for this compendium. If ever a "book" evolved unplanned, this is it. The random collection of insights on human nature began nearly a quarter of a century ago; and it was never intended for publication. For much of that time, they remained highlighted phrases on the pages of the books in which I found them. As the number of these "phrases" grew over the years, a number of startling insights started to emerge. Four of those insights are the reasons why I eventually decided to compile and share this compendium and, soon, its sequel. The "reasons" are:

Sobering reminders of who we truly are as humans, bringing us face-to-face with our innermost and essential nature as humans.

Vitally important clues to the understanding and realistic resolution of many of the psychological, social, and economic crises humanity is facing.

(Potentially) foundational idea in the crucial and increasingly urgent task of transforming the way we perceive ourselves, raise children, educate the youth, govern society, manage institutions and organizations, give care, and relate with one another and with the rest of nature.

New paradigm for thinking about ourselves – a radically new and authentic concept of human nature which is likely to intrigue, challenge, and engage social scientists and social philosophers for some time to come.

I am confident that the authentic new understanding of human nature that is uncovered in this compendium will inform efforts to build a global society in which all the Earth's estimated seven billion inhabitants are able to develop and to contribute their special abilities in important and beneficial actions and, thus, to experience their lives as having meaning and significance.

ALPHABETICAL COMPENDIUM

OF

1,771

REVEALING

AND

CONVERGING

INSIGHTS

ON

HUMAN NATURE

AND

CREATIVITY

"It is highly important, indeed urgently so, that we consider the possibility that our traditional ideas concerning the innate nature of man may be wrong and damaging, for I am convinced that underlying much of man's malfunctioning … is this unsound conception of human nature."

Ashley Montagu

0001
"a biological a priori"

0002
"a boundless treasure of goodness … inherent in [us] all"

0003
"a call into the fullness of life"

0004
"a call to our deepest self to come forward"

0005
"a calling from life itself"

0006
"a cause for which you have great passion"

0007
"a cause in which one can believe and to which one can be dedicated"

0008
"a cause you are committed to, a local service project that could use your help … [where] your energies and ideas can make a difference – in your life and your world"

0009
"a center out of which you act"

0010
"a central core of being human"

Let each become all that he was created capable of being.

Aristotle

0011
"a characteristic pattern of potentials each of us displays [sic]"

0012
"a child's inborn nature"

0013
"a coherent purpose … a harmonious theme in the apparent chaos of experience"

0014
"a core longing in our soul"

0015
"a deep human urge – to explore, to create, to discover, to achieve, to change, to improve"

0016
"a deep, inner, compulsive – almost primal – drive … to leave an indelible imprint on the world"

0017
"a deeper aspect of ourselves, ordinarily dormant, asleep, unused"

0018
"a deeper call in our lives"

0019
"a deeper, more profound part of our beings"

0020
"a deeper purpose, one that involves being present with ourselves and, in so doing, bringing some aspect of the world to life"

All of history supports the observation that the desire to create is a fundamental urge in humankind.

Willis Harman and John Hormann

0021
"a deeper sense of life purpose"

0022
"a defining image"

0023
"a definite aim and model for life"

0024
"a desire to put something back … to contribute"

0025
"a desire within the heart of every person [sic] to be a source oneself of the revelation we have received"

0026
"a difficult enough goal from which all other goals logically follow … [in the pursuit of which] the separate parts of a person's life will fit together"

0027
"a dimension of existence beyond that experienced through the senses [sic]"

0028
"a divine dimension, a bit of God's image in every one of us"

0029
"a driving force in each of our lives"

0030
"a fact of nature which cannot be abolished"

True happiness involves the full use of one's powers and talents.

John W. Gardner

0031
"a flowcr blooming from lifc"

0032
"a fulfillment need that many are experiencing … a deeper sense of life purpose"

0033
"a fulfillment whose limits extend to infinity"

0034
"a fully human, fully alive existence"

0035
"a fundamental human essence that, where uninhibited, has found expression in all societies and cultures at all times"

0036
"a gift from the gods which makes [you] unique"

0037
"a gnawing and unfaltering human hunger"

0038
"a goal that brings harmony to a person's life"

0039
"a gold mine within you from which you can extract everything you need to live life gloriously, joyously, and abundantly"

0040
"a grand purpose to life or for an individual soul"

Everyone is born a genius.
Society degeniuses them.

Buckminster Fuller

0041
"a great force in our life for good or evil, depending on what we have chosen"

0042
"a growing edge, the part of us that goes beyond what we believe to be possible"

0043
"a higher level of consciousness [that] guides [sic] our actions"

0044
"a higher level of humanity"

0045
"a human being doing what she or he was meant to do"

0046
"a hunger that will never be satisfied with any created thing"

0047
"a life filled with meaning and passion"

0048
"[a] life task devotion to [which] raises [one] above the pettiness and paltriness that necessarily devour meaningless lives"

0049
"a life task set by God"

0050
"a life [we] can feel good about"

Creative talent is a widely distributed gift …
… an ability that need not wane with age.

Alex F. Osborn

0051
“a magical ability to change the world [that] each of us has”

0052
“a man’s individual nature”

0053
“a man’s true nature”

0054
“a meaning we all have [sic] to fulfill”

0055
“a melting of our work into the great work of the universe”

0056
“[a message] that you have been chosen by the universe to receive”

0057
“a more spiritual and truly human way of living”

0058
“a more transcendent dimension of life”

0059
“a mysterious a sense of transcendence, of universal harmony [that] certain activities … produce [sic]”

0060
“a natural ability that we are all endowed with”

How shall I live so that my life will mean something more than a brief flash of biological existence soon to disappear forever?

Harold Kushner

0061

"a natural and powerful urge that everyone's life, regardless of culture, obeys"

0062

"a natural desire and capacity to contribute to life"

0063

"a natural endowment of all humanity"

0064

"a natural tendency towards complete development in man"

0065

"a natural urge for growth and fulfillment"

0066

"a need that is universal and timeless"

0067

"a new and enduring wholeness and beauty – a renewed relationship of man to himself, to other men, to society, to nature, and to the land"

0068

"a new kind of work that awaits us and is demanded of us"

0069

"a new point of view that had not been previously considered"

0070

"a part of ourselves that knows the way to health, wholeness and success"

One of the idiosyncratic needs inherent in the human organism is the need to create, to bring order out of chaos.

Berenice Bleedorn

0071
"a part that each of us has [sic] in nurturing this interconnected whole and healing it where it is torn"

0072
"a particular image by which [sic] each life is formed, an image that is the essence of that life and calls it to a destiny"

0073
"a person's directional tendencies"

0074
"a person's intimate sensations of truth"

0075
"a personal pursuit of truth"

0076
"a place for ourselves in a mighty universe"

0077
"a place in every man's being where he is one with all that is because he is one with the universal Spirit which is in all that is"

0078
"a point where our external labors and the opus of the soul are one and the same"

0079
"a powerful potential force"

0080
"a preexisting capacity that an [individual] possesses from birth"

By tapping his full measure of creative intelligence, an individual may begin to reflect humanity's highest ideals in his life. ... Such individual development offers the key to solving modern man's social problems.

Harold H. Bloomfield

0081
"a primal human motive and a timeless source of physiologic strength and health"

0082
"a process of unfolding that is not entirely of my own making"

0083
"a profound need to be of genuine service to the agencies for which we work, to be truly useful, even essential, in our jobs"

0084
"a progressive tendency, a movement toward fulfillment [that] all life exhibits"

0085
"a prompter which … indicates the direction in which we have to move in a given life situation"

0086
"a quality innate in each individual … potentially in limitless supply"

0087
"a question that will offer you a lifetime of pondering, that will lead you toward what you need to know for your integrity"

0088
"a quiet voice [that is pointing] you in the direction that you want to go [which] if you forget to notice, your life can get out of control"

0089
"a real and authentic sense of self-worth"

0090
"a relationship between the person and some larger system of ideas or values, a relationship involving obligations as well as rewards"

Creativity is God-given; born into each of us. It
is not an oddity, but a
naturalness long neglected.

George R. Eckstein

0091

"a relationship with life that is both materially and spiritually satisfying"

0092

"a response to the call to choose life [sic] … to opt for a future for our planet, for our children and theirs, and for all the species that render this planet so amazing and so beautiful"

0093

"a return to our origins"

0094

"a reunion with the laws of life"

0095

"[a] right which each person expresses as a direct prerogative from the Infinite Will and Consciousness"

0096

"a role each of us has to play [sic] in shaping what lies ahead"

0097

"a search for infinite beauty, a search for Spirit"

0098

"a search for that one note that had truth and meaning, the one note that I could claim … was truly my own"

0099

"a selfhood based on the development of individual potential"

0100

"a sense of being part of the great all-inclusive life [that] prompts us to reflect on our own place and on how we ought to live"

The human heart is restless unless he has found, and fulfilled, meaning and purpose in life. … There is nothing in the world … that would so effectively help one to survive even the worst conditions as the knowledge that there is a meaning in one's life.

Viktor E. Frankl

0101
"a sense of exhilaration that floods the self [sic] when we undertake a task that requires complex skills, that leads to a challenging goal"

0102
"a sense of [one's] own unique individuality"

0103
"a sense of oneness with other beings and [the] desire to heal society"

0104
"a sense of personal calling, that there is a reason I am alive"

0105
"a sense of ultimate purpose"

0106
"a significant vehicle for speeding the evolution of human intellect and consciousness to a higher level"

0107
"a source of deep energy"

0108
"a special character and fate – qualities of soul – each individual has [sic] that must be safeguarded even at the risk of losing ordinary assurances of safety and normality"

0109
"a special purpose waiting to be lived"

0110
"a special story each person has to tell [sic], no matter how many common themes it contains"

The belief that creativity is limited to artists is dangerous and costly. It stops many people who work outside of the arts from using their creative abilities, since they believe they don't have any ...

Derm Barrett

0111
"a specific calling that belongs inescapably to you"

0112
"[a] specific vocation or mission in life that [sic] everybody has to carry out – [sic] a concrete assignment which demands fulfillment. Therein he cannot be replaced, nor his life repeated"

0113
"a spiritual reason for being that all people have [sic] and that our world is incomplete until each one of us discovers [his or her own]"

0114
"a state of being in which one is free to do what one wants for its own sake and its own end"

0115
"a story living in us that speaks of our place in the world … a story that invites us to love what we love and simply to be ourselves"

0116
"a strong sense of individuality – personal destiny, special influences and background, and unique stories"

0117
"a system of meanings that gives purpose to one's being"

0118
"a talent that is unique in its expression; so unique that there's no one else alive on this planet that has that talent"

0119
"a tendency toward, or need for, growing in a direction that can be summarized … as self-actualization or psychological health"

0120
"a thirst for meaning that cannot be filled with ordinary activities and accomplishments"

Creativity is not a you have it or you don't proposition. It is a continuum and a fundamental attribute of all humanity.

Ross Webber

0121
"a true pathway for the soul"

0122
"a unified purpose that gives meaning to a person's life"

0123
"a unifying sense of direction [that] can withstand much stress and is actually strengthened by overcoming difficulties"

0124
"a unique mission in life"

0125
"a uniqueness that each person bears [sic] that seeks to be lived"

0126
"a very definite conception of what [one] is living for"

0127
"a virtually unlimited source of energy and intelligence"

0128
"a vital force and fundamental tendency of the human personality"

0129
"a vocation, a calling from a place that is the source of meaning and identity, the roots of which lie beyond human intention and interpretation"

0130
"a voice from within which we all possess"

Man has to solve a problem, he can never rest
in the given situation
of a passive adaptation to nature.

Erich Fromm

0131
"a way of life that enables both the self and others to enjoy happiness and peace ... the life of great good to create value for society"

0132
"a wellspring of health"

0133
"a will to meaning in contrast to the pleasure principle"

0134
"a wonderful and tenacious internal guidance system for individual transformation"

0135
"a work connected to the origins of the universe [wherein] lies its dignity; [wherein] lies its power; [wherein] lies its reward"

0136
"a work mission that goes beyond ourselves"

0137
"ability for making something new out of old situations and resources"

0138
"ability to express what [we are] gifted to do"

0139
"ability to see what others overlook"

0140
"[ability] to fulfill [our] destiny as human beings"

Your suppressed potentialities will make you miserable.

Bertrand Russell

0141
"ability to sense the world in [one's] own unique way"

0142
"achieving success with fulfillment"

0143
"acting out our being"

0144
"act[ion] at the peak of [our] capacity [that] both improves subjective well-being and has the potential for socially positive consequences"

0145
"actions that lead to greater harmony within ourselves, society, and the broader environment of which we are a part"

0146
"activities that truly engage us with ourselves and others"

0147
"activities which are of the most interest and the most fulfilling"

0148
"actualizing the potential meaning of one's [sic] life"

0149
"add[ing] something of value to the world"

0150
"align[ing] our identity with [the] larger pattern"

To be nobody but yourself in a world which is doing its best, night and day, to make you everybody else, means to fight the hardest battle which any human being can fight; and never stop fighting.

ee. cummings

0151
"align[ing] with the power that manifests everything in the universe"

0152
"align[ing] yourself with your soul instead of with your personality"

0153
"alignment with the universe itself"

0154
"all our efforts to grow, to develop, and to contribute"

0155
"all that is human in man"

0156
"allowing our authentic human nature to express itself"

0157
"an active will toward health, an impulse toward growth, or toward the actualization of human potentialities"

0158
"an all-encompassing goal that prescribes [sic] a specific pattern of behavior to follow until death … a purpose that extends beyond the grave"

0159
"an awakening of our bodies' natural frequency upward toward resonance with the universal frequency of love"

0160
"an awakening of the Higher Self"

The ultimate disease of our time is valuelessness ... rootlessness, emptiness, helplessness, the lack of something to believe in and to be devoted to. … No psychological health is possible unless [the] essential core of the person is fundamentally accepted, loved and respected by others and by himself.

Abraham H. Maslow

0161
"an essential part of your personhood"

0162
"an essentially human quality"

0163
"an eternal aspect of human nature"

0164
"an eternal process of being and becoming"

0165
"an explosive force within all people [sic] ready to be unleashed into the world"

0166
"an expression of our soul, our inner being"

0167
"an imagination which must be used and enjoyed in order for [man] to experience the complete fulfillment of life"

0168
"an impelling life-force … which gives rise to the ever-new face of manifest creation"

0169
"an imprisoned splendor"

0170
"an 'inner calling,' a voice from within stating that the way to make a difference in the world is to be helpful to others"

There is increasing scientific evidence that man's physical and psychological health are profoundly affected by the degree to which he has found meaning, direction, and purpose in his existence. … A person lives as long as he experiences his life as having meaning and value and as long as he has something to live for – meaningful projects that inspirit him and invite him to move into his future. … As soon as meaning, value and hope vanish from a person's experience, he begins to stop living; he begins to die.

Sidney M. Jourard

0171
"an incredible wisdom that often appears like Divine inspiration"

0172
"an indispensable condition in the quest for personal fulfillment"

0173
"an individual's search for a meaning"

0174
"an individual's specific character and destiny"

0175
"an inescapable [human] tendency"

0176
"an inexhaustible source of intelligence [and] energy … that exists throughout creation and in every human being … that can be logically explained, scientifically verified, artistically actualized … and systematically drawn upon by everyone for spontaneous use in all kinds of … activity"

0177
"an inmost center in us all, where truth abides in fullness … and to know rather consists in opening out a way whence the imprisoned splendour may escape, than in effecting entry for a light supposed to be without"

0178
"an innate, human impulse to discover what is purposeful about life"

0179
"an inner compass that gives [our] lives meaning and structure"

0180
"an inner creature of conscience whose insistent voice brooks no disobedience"

Humans ultimately seek meaning, not comfort; creative work, not inactivity. … Much business practice is still oriented around outdated theories of motivation which assume that people are motivated by money, power, status, or a hierarchy of needs.

Willis Harman and John Hormann

0181
"an inner dimension to our work"

0182
"an inner dynamic that gives the feeling of purpose to occasions"

0183
"an inner greatness we call our own"

0184
"an inner need"

0185
"an inner urge for progress"

0186
"an inner vitality that has a life and momentum of its own"

0187
"an inner voice one recognizes as wiser than one's own"

0188
"an inner voice that tells us to be caring, not cruel"

0189
"an internal sense of meaning and impact"

0190
"an invariant human propensity"

Everyone of us can bring phenomenal possibilities into actuality – in transcending circumstances and recreating our lives, our families, our organizations, and our society.

George Land and Beth Jarman

0191
"an invisible but living reality"

0192
"an offering of life"

0193
"an invisible, intangible, yet fundamental reality, from which life flows forth, and the effects of which we perceive indirectly in the tangible reality which is accessible to scientific study"

0194
"an opportunity to cooperate with the universe, to be part of what the Chinese call the great river of the Tao"

0195
"an ultimate thirst of our souls"

0196
"an underlying ... movement towards constructive fulfillment of [one's] inherent possibilities"

0197
"an untold story inside you"

0198
"another part of myself, one that is in intimate contact with the dance of creation that surrounds me"

0199
"another place from which my knowing could come"

0200
"areas of [our] maximum potential"

The life of the individual only has meaning in so far as it aids in making the life of every living thing nobler and more beautiful.

Albert Einstein

0201
"aspects of the awesome order which we find in the universe as a whole"

0202
"authentic being"

0203
"authentic living"

0204
"authentic power – the alignment of personality with the soul"

0205
"authentic selfhood"

0206
"authentic spiritual purpose"

0207
"authentic work [that] connects us to the creative habits of the universe"

0208
"authenticity of living"

0209
"awakening to our soul and life purpose"

0210
"awakening to the original need of one's soul"

I believe there is little question that prolonged, enforced repression of the creative desire may lead to actual breakdown of the personality.

E. Paul Torrance

0211
"awaken[ing] to the true joy of purposeful living"

0212
"awareness of the one work of the universe and our relation to it"

0213
"basic inclinations"

0214
"basic inner purposes"

0215
"basic needs in the human psyche"

0216
"becoming active partner [sic] in the construction of the future"

0217
"becoming all you can become"

0218
"becom[ing] at one with the power that is the universe"

0219
"becoming fully who we are by doing fully what we do"

0220
"becoming joint citizens of a cosmos where we learn from other creatures"

Regardless of how he expresses his problem, everyone who needs psychiatric treatment suffers from one basic inadequacy: he is unable to fulfill his essential needs.

William Glasser

0221
"becom[ing] one with the Divine Truth"

0222
"becoming [one's] own uniqueness"

0223
"becom[ing] part of the stream of evolution"

0224
"becoming the most that we can be psychospiritually"

0225
"becoming the person you are, however peculiar that may be"

0226
"becoming what [one] should be"

0227
"becoming what we can and ought to be"

0228
"becom[ing] what we really [sic] are and can be"

0229
"[being] called to greatness"

0230
"being fully present in life"

In our attempt to improve the world, have we been fighting the smoke instead of the fire - the symptoms instead of the disease? ... If it could be found that the problems before us have one common source, and if that source could be located and eliminated, the problem could be eradicated in one stroke, just as turning on the light puts an immediate end to the darkness of a room.

Jack Forem

0231
"being in harmony with an unseen order of things"

0232
"being in the world soulfully"

0233
"[being] in touch with the purposes and patterns of life"

0234
"be[ing] open to the whole human experience"

0235
"be[ing] ready to be questioned by life"

0236
"being what no other can exactly be, and [doing] what no other can exactly do"

0237
"belief [sic] that our lives will make a difference for someone or for something"

0238
"birthing our deepest images"

0239
"blending with life … living in harmony with the natural cycles"

0240
"boundless potentialities – the noble bodhisattva life-condition – [sic] that everybody possesses"

We fail more often because we solve the wrong problem than because we get the wrong solution to the right problem.

R. L. Ackoff

0241

"breaking through the established order to do the thing never done before, never anticipated by the guardians of orderliness"

0242

"bring[ing] forth possibilities that seemed never to have existed"

0243

"bringing something new and worthwhile into the world"

0244

"bringing spirit and livelihood back together again"

0245

"building a self in harmony with the universal order … recogniz[ing] our kinship with the rest of creation"

0246

"careful meshing of human purposes with the larger patterns and flows of the natural world and the study of those patterns and flows to inform human purposes"

0247

"categorical desires that give us reasons for living"

0248

"central loyalty"

0249

"choos[ing] our life purpose and exist[ing] according to that purpose"

0250

"connect[ing] our daily lives to the Great Work of the universe"

There is every reason to believe that the social ills at present afflicting … society – increasing crime, delinquency, vandalism, alcoholism, as well as drug addiction – are closely related and are the symptoms of the breakdown of our cultural pattern, which in turn is an aspect of the disintegration of our society. … It is chimeric to suppose that any of these tendencies can be checked … by treating them in isolation apart from the social disease of which they are but the symptoms. It is the cause itself … that must be treated.

Edward Goldsmith *et al.*

0251
"connect[ing] the outer field of activity with the unbounded potentiality of the inner man, for the purpose of enriching all"

0252
"connection to one's genuine and authentic being"

0253
"connection to some higher purpose or calling"

0254
"connecting with the innate wisdom within me [sic]"

0255
"connecting with the Oneness of it all"

0256
"continuous quest for wholeness"

0257
"contributing to a purpose outside of and larger than [oneself]"

0258
"contribut[ing] to the constructive plan of life itself"

0259
"cooperating with the cycles of nature"

0260
"core commitment that gives life meaning"

Man has been endowed with a creative mind,
whether or not he knows it.

Ernest Holmes

0261

"creating new possibilities for our world"

0262

"deep inner trait that we all have (but almost never recognize or act upon)"

0263

"deeper and enduring concerns of the soul"

0264

"developing [and contributing one's] intellectual and artistic powers to whatever extent accords with [one's] personal characteristics and abilities"

0265

"different roles for different souls … a distinct personality or way of dealing with life's challenges that [sic] everybody has"

0266

"discovering and following [the] rich musical images hidden beneath the keys … that filled me with the most joy"

0267

"discovering and fulfilling your destiny"

0268

"discovering and living your soul's purpose"

0269

"discovering, developing, and nurturing what fulfills the deepest part of you"

0270

"discovering our core values and honoring them [sic]"

All life is one. The world is one home.
All are members of one human family.
All creation is an organic whole.
No Man is independent of this whole.
Man makes himself miserable by separating
himself from others.
Separation is death.
Unity is eternal life.

Sivananda

0271
"discovering our God-given gifts and potential ... and then developing [sic] them"

0272
"discover[ing] [our] purpose and express[ing] [our] calling"

0273
"discovering what our individual contribution can be, then giving ourselves fully to it"

0274
"discover[ing] who [one] is and what [one] may become"

0275
"displaying the beautiful, displaying our being, displaying our truth, displaying life, and therefore displaying God, the life giver"

0276
"divine light burning in [our] personalities and [our] actions"

0277
"divine mode of being"

0278
"domain-specific predispositions ... embedded a priori in the [individual]"

0279
"each in our own way ... act[ing] with wisdom and grace, bringing greater harmony to the planet"

0280
"each life's compass toward divine reunion with its Creator"

Life cannot be divided up into neat little
packages of
physical,
emotional,
intellectual,
and
spiritual.
Our world doesn't break into finely-drawn
segments of
social,
political,
economic,
and
religious.
Whether we recognize it or not, there is an integration in life which brings all of the various parts and experiences together into a single entity.

Arthur Beals

0281
"each man's [sic] own view of the world"

0282
"each [of us being] a part of the emerging chorus, whose collective voice may reawaken the sense of longing and wonder that slumbers still and, in so doing, dissolve some of the layers of doubt and fear that separate us from the fertile ground from which all life comes"

0283
"each of us following a deeper call"

0284
"each [of us] wanting and working for the true happiness of all"

0285
"encounter with the artistic part of my nature and listening closely to what it was that it wanted to say"

0286
"enduring motivation [that comes] ultimately from within the individual"

0287
"enduring wisdom and power"

0288
"enjoyment that comes from surpassing ourselves, from mastering new obstacles"

0289
"enter[ing] into a flowing relationship with life [and] stay[ing] connected with this flow"

0290
"eternal work [that] truly springs from our inner self and our ground"

For the person with creative potential, there is no wholeness except in using it.

Robert K. Greenleaf

0291
"everyone's [sic] own specific vocation or mission in life"

0292
"everything that is human on earth"

0293
"existential fulfillment"

0294
"existential necessity"

0295
"exploring [our] inner being and expressing it"

0296
"exploiting [sic] our unique potentials to become extraordinary in our own right"

0297
"expressing your talent to fulfill needs"

0298
"[expression of] our own highest values"

0299
"fan[ning] into flame that fragile ember that burns quietly in my own soul [sic]"

0300
"feel[ling] compelled to share [our] inner truth"

The aim of life is the unfolding of man's creative powers.

Erich Fromm

0301
"feel[ing] deeply connected to ourselves and to something bigger than ourselves"

0302
"feelings of destiny"

0303
"feeling of extreme involvement and pleasure"

0304
"feeling of transcendence"

0305
"feelings of uniqueness, of grandeur … the restlessness of the heart, its impatience, its dissatisfaction, its yearning"

0306
"feelings that the world somehow wants me to be here"

0307
"final causes (that for the sake of which we do things)"

0308
"find[ing] a beacon toward which we can steer the boat"

0309
"finding a meaning in life"

0310
"finding a perspective that no one else has taken, acting on your newly found knowledge, and then seeing the contribution that your efforts make to the betterment"

The innumerable problems of the world are due to lack of contact with [the] unbounded field of creative intelligence. The specific individual problems are only symptoms of a deeper disease, and it is time to stop treating the symptoms and begin to deal directly with the underlying ailment.

Maharishi Mahesh Yogi

0311
"finding and following an authentic life"

0312
"finding [and following] your passion"

0313
"finding and giving ourselves"

0314
"finding and living what you were born to do"

0315
"finding and living your purpose in life … becoming the person you were born to be"

0316
"finding fulfillment from doing what you were born to do"

0317
"finding my own way"

0318
"find[ing] one's [sic] place and fulfill[ing] one's [sic] part of the overall purpose of existence"

0319
"find[ing] something big to live for"

0320
"find[ing] the cause that moves us and the role that fits our most unique gifts"

What is originality? To see something that has no name as yet and hence cannot be mentioned although it stares us all in the face. The way men usually are, it takes a name to make something visible for them.

Friedrich Nietzsche

0321
"finding the fulfillment you're missing … creat[ing] and liv[ing] your vision of success"

0322
"finding what [your] real work is and doing it"

0323
"finding your own path"

0324
"flash of insight that takes us beyond ourselves … [in which moment] of inspiration [sic] we transcend our separateness, become one with all life"

0325
"[flow] feelings – which include concentration, absorption, deep involvement, joy, a sense of accomplishment – [that] people describe as the best moments in their lives [and that] can occur almost anywhere, at any time, provided one is using psychic energy in a harmonious pattern"

0326
"focus so clear that little else matters outside that awareness"

0327
"following [our] own interests … becoming the person [we are] meant to be"

0328
"follow[ing] our own souls"

0329
"following the underlying principles that support life … creating [sic] a healthier, more peaceful life for ourselves and our world"

0330
"free[dom] to develop a self to the utmost level of its potential complexity, but not … curtail another person's freedom to do so"

Capacities clamor to be used, and cease their clamor only when they are well used. … The unused skill or capacity or organ can become a disease center or else atrophy or disappear, thus diminishing the person.

Abraham H. Maslow

0331
"fulfilling [one's] sense of purpose"

0332
"fulfilling our natures as human beings"

0333
"fulfill[ing] our purpose as human being"

0334
"fulfillment of soul in service to life"

0335
"fulfillment of transcendental needs"

0336
"fulfillment – the realization of inherent capacities by the individual and of new possibilities by the race"

0337
"full possibility of the human being"

0338
"fundamental drive of all living things"

0339
"fundamental to human nature"

0340
"genetic instruction … the information encoded in our genes"

It is an indignity for any human being not to be allowed to live up to his or her full potential.

Hazel Henderson

0341
"get[ting] back in touch with who you really are … reconnection with the part of yourself that can direct the fulfillment of your purpose in life"

0342
"getting beyond the boxes we call disciplines to see things in their ecological context"

0343
"[getting] in touch with the resources [we] need – and already own – in order to function effectively and fulfill [our] lives"

0344
"getting in touch with the spiritual side of your nature"

0345
"giv[ing] form to the life that rises up from within us … giv[ing] our own voice to the world"

0346
"giving our gifts to … something we believe in"

0347
"gifts and abilities we are not using and need to put to work"

0348
"goals that are so persuasive that they justify effort even when our resources are exhausted and when fate is merciless in refusing us a chance at having a comfortable life"

0349
"God-given talents of mind, heart, and imagination"

0350
"God's will for each of us"

In every organization, most people conceive new ideas worth fashioning into innovations. But most of these ideas are never born. Of the new ideas that are born, most die soon after birth. And of the ideas that do live, most are trampled to death in infancy or fail to achieve maturity to carry through into an effective innovation.

Marvin Bower

0351
"godlike potentialities"

0352
"going out of ourselves [sic] in genuine caring and concern for others"

0353
"good work … the practice of ecological virtue"

0354
"great vision that comes from beyond the personality"

0355
"growing longing to exceed ourselves, to be more than we are ordinarily defined"

0356
"grow[ing] to your full potential"

0357
"growth tendency … a drive toward self-actualization … the urge which is evident in all organic and human life – to expand, extend, become autonomous, develop, mature – the tendency to express and activate all the capacities of the organism"

0358
"habits of mind that seek out 'patterns that connect' human and natural systems"

0359
"harmonizing [sic] human artifacts and systems … with the larger patterns in which they are embedded"

0360
"harmonizing with the natural cycles of the world"

All social functions are equally necessary, and those that perform them are hence equally deserving of respect.

Jonathan Gershuny

0361
"harmony with life"

0362
"hear[ing] the still small voice that calls you by name"

0363
"helping others by working on purpose"

0364
"hidden assets buried within your soul and long forgotten"

0365
"higher calling"

0366
"higher human power"

0367
"higher motivations"

0368
"higher order psychological need"

0369
"higher order synthesis"

0370
"higher purpose ... a yearning for something greater than money and material possessions"

Everybody ought to feel that whatever his or her calling, they can be excellent.

John W. Gardner

0371
"how I am best suited to serve humanity"

0372
"how [I am to] live so that my life will mean something more than a brief flash of biological existence soon to disappear forever"

0373
"how to be a human being"

0374
"how to live so that our lives matter, so that the world will be at least a little bit different for our having passed through it"

0375
"how we can help [sic] to realize the potential inherent in the cosmos"

0376
"human nature"

0377
"human needs for purpose, meaning, and significance"

0378
"human objectives [sic] which lie outside the commercial standards … objectives which are generally assigned a second place or altogether neglected by ordinary commercial practice"

0379
"human possibilities"

0380
"human purpose"

There is as much dignity in tilling a field as in writing a poem.

Booker T. Washington

0381
"humanity's potential for evolving consciousness, empathy and altruism"

0382
"humanity's tremendous untapped inner potential"

0383
"hunger for higher being"

0384
"identifying with the cosmic evolution"

0385
"identif[ication] with the larger processes at work in the cosmos"

0386
"images that ignite your imagination and expand your field of possibilities"

0387
"immeasurable power within you"

0388
"immense innate knowledge in the human that we would all consider to be spiritual knowledge, but … that we don't know how to access it and cultivate it in the present global context"

0389
"impelling life force"

0390
"important gifts each of us has [sic] to share with the world"

Do we live only to produce children, to perpetuate the human race? And having done that, is it our destiny to disappear and make way for the next generation? Or is there a purpose to our existence beyond simply existing? Does our being alive matter? Would our disappearance leave the world poorer, or just less crowded?

Harold Kushner

0391
"incorporating intelligence about how nature works into the way we think, design, build, and live"

0392
"individual ego maturation to self-actualizing transcendent awareness"

0393
"individual patterns in human growth"

0394
"individual soulhood"

0395
"individuality, the striving of each person to be unique and to realize his or her full powers and potentials"

0396
"individualized soul-image"

0397
"infinite human possibilities"

0398
"infinite life … expressing itself through me"

0399
"inherent possibilities"

0400
"innate abilities"

Creative individuals don't have to be dragged out of bed; they are eager to start the day. This is not because they are cheerful, enthusiastic types. Nor do they necessarily have something exciting to do. But they believe that there is something meaningful to accomplish each day, and they can't wait to get started on it. Most of us don't feel our actions are that meaningful. Yet everyone can discover at least one thing every day that is worth waking up for.

Mihaly Csikszentmihalyi

0401
"innate character"

0402
"innate human impulse to discover what is purposeful about life"

0403
"innate image"

0404
"innate potentialities that shape [people's] ends and direct the lines of their individual development and growth"

0405
"innate power [that] will inevitably find its way into the light [though] we try taming and boxing [it] in"

0406
"innate striving for meaning"

0407
"innate striving for sanity"

0408
"inner compulsion ... something which unless you do it, you don't really feel you are living"

0409
"inner disposition of man"

0410
"inner drive for excellence"

Am I living in a way which is deeply satisfying to me, and which truly expresses me? That … is perhaps the most important question for the creative individual.

Carl R. Rogers

0411
"inner dynamism of life: the tendency to grow, to be expressed, to be lived"

0412
"inner essence"

0413
"inner force that compels behavior"

0414
"inner glory"

0415
"inner guidance"

0416
"inner hunger to know who we are at the soul level and to participate in the grandeur of the universe"

0417
"inner motivation to stay on a particular path"

0418
"inner nature"

0419
"inner necessity"

0420
"inner purpose"

Without some cause in which to lose themselves, some creed in which to find themselves, or some loved object of value for which to sacrifice themselves, men live lives without point and purpose.

Cyril E. M. Joad

0421
"inner reality"

0422
"inner resource of thought, a reservoir of 'unlimited energy, intelligence, power, peace and bliss'"

0423
"inner source of thought"

0424
"inner spark"

0425
"inner urge to grow and to develop [according to one's endowment]"

0426
"inner work that men have neglected for far too long"

0427
"innermost storehouse of intelligence and energy"

0428
"interexisten[ce] with all beings"

0429
"internal oracle whose injunctions [we need to follow]"

0430
"intrinsic motivation to do something for its own sake, the motivation to undertake an activity because it is interesting, enjoyable, satisfying, or personally challenging"

A life is meaningless if it lacks active engagement with, subjective attraction to, or an affinity for any worthwhile thing(s), if it has no desires that give a person a reason to live. A person who is bored or alienated from most of what she spends her life doing is one who can be said to lack meaning …even though she may in fact be performing functions of worth [sic.].

Susan Wolf

0431
"intuitive experience which leads most directly to a sense of well-being and harmony with oneself and the universe"

0432
"intuitive guidance from within"

0433
"invest[ing] [one's] psychic energy in the most universal goals … goals that transcend [one's] narrow interests"

0434
"join[ing] in the celebration of life"

0435
"joining the dance of Creation"

0436
"join[ing] with [all of creation] now in what was the first song of humanity, the joyful cry, 'I am!'"

0437
"labor and devotion to one's mission [that alone] give life its worth"

0438
"labor that is profound repose"

0439
"labors of the soul"

0440
"latent possibilities"

The value of life lies not in the length of days, but in the use we make of them; a man may live long yet live very little.

Michel E. Montaigne

0441
"leading a life that allows me to [be and] like myself"

0442
"learn[ing] to believe in someone or something so deeply that life is charged with meaning and a sense of mission"

0443
"let[ting] our stored-up benevolence … [our] untapped goodness [sic] flow more abundantly during our normal daily activities [and] bring world healing to our ailing society"

0444
"life-giving roles"

0445
"life seeking expression through action"

0446
"[life's] inherent tendency to grow, to expand, to express potentialities"

0447
"life's intrinsic desire to express itself"

0448
"life's ultimate purpose"

0449
"limitless self-perfection"

0450
"listen[ing] to the soul's voice and follow[ing] its call"

Everyone must learn to believe in …
something so deeply that life is charged with
meaning and a sense of mission.

John Powell

0451
"listen[ing] to the truth of our experience and then utter[ing] it in simple symbols and expressions … putting it into form, articulating it for others to behold and to criticize"

0452
"listening to the voice of the soul"

0453
"living a healthier life of mind, body, and spirit while deepening connections to self, family, community, environment, and planet"

0454
"living a specific mission for which we as souls came into the world"

0455
"living at one with our wisest self"

0456
"living authentically, according to our true character"

0457
"liv[ing] growingly and … respond[ing] to the rhythm of life itself"

0458
"living humanly"

0459
"living in a fully functioning way"

0460
"living in depth, living with meaning, purpose, joy, and a sense of contributing to the greater community"

Everybody is different. Everybody has something to give that nobody else in the world has. Isn't that enough for you to become enthusiastic about yourself? And also, to say to yourself, My goodness, I've got to find out what that is.

Leo Buscaglia

0461
"living in harmony with the universe … living life as it was meant to be lived"

0462
"liv[ing] in partnership with the natural current of things [sic],
feel[ing] at one with the rocks, and the water, and the pines"

0463
"living out a calling"

0464
"living out our life purpose with passion"

0465
"living realities … which are still at work in our hearts, and which fashion our person"

0466
"living the simple truth of who [we] are"

0467
"living to some purpose"

0468
"liv[ing] up to increasingly complex images of our selves"

0469
"living what we love"

0470
"living your mission in life"

Nothing is more natural to human beings than to be inventive and creative.

Derm Barrett

0471
"living your passion"

0472
"living your spiritual purposes"

0473
"locked treasure chest … hidden assets buried within your soul and long forgotten"

0474
"mak[ing] the invisible visible"

0475
"making the life of every living thing nobler and more beautiful"

0476
"[making] the world a better place, a happier place, and a more human place because [one] lived … here"

0477
"man as nature made him"

0478
"man's capacity to rise above his outward fate"

0479
"man's capacity to transcend his predicament and discover an adequate guiding truth"

0480
"man's created nature"

Each man has his vocation.

Ralph Waldo Emerson

0481
"[man's] deeper meaning [which] lies in the whole of which he is inescapably a part"

0482
"man's essential nature"

0483
"man's hunger for dedication … directed to worthy objects"

0484
"man's inalienable, relentless drive to question"

0485
"man's inner greatness"

0486
"man's inner nature"

0487
"man's … inner needs"

0488
"man's most important characteristic"

0489
"man's motives and goals … the measure of man"

0490
"[man's] place in the scheme of things"

Everyone has his own specific vocation or mission in life; everyone must carry out a concrete assignment that demands fulfillment. Therein he cannot be replaced, nor can his life be repeated. Thus everyone's task is unique as his special opportunity to implement it.

Viktor E. Frankl

0491
"man's primary motivational force"

0492
"man's [sic] search for identity … and a personally satisfying meaning to life"

0493
"man's search for meaning [which] is the primary motivation in his life"

0494
"man's spiritual nature and … his relationship to the Infinite"

0495
"man's tendency to actualize himself, to become his potentialities"

0496
"man's vitality [that] shows itself not simply as a biological force, but as a reaching out, a forming and re-forming of the world in various creative activities"

0497
"manifesting [our] individualities fully instead of being jealous and emulative of one another … manifesting individuality within an awareness of coalition [while] recognizing the individuality of all other members of the coalition"

0498
"mankind as a whole … on the 'path of return' [or] reintegration into that of which he was at one time an unconscious part, and later an estranged and prodigal son – reintegration into planetary life"

0499
"mankind's eternal quest to evolve to an ever higher self-fulfillment"

0500
"mankind's most important adaptability skills"

Each person is a creative being capable of bringing into existence what has never been before.

George Land and Beth Jarman

0501
"mankind's ultimate capital asset"

0502
"many kinds of excellence at many levels"

0503
"meaningful and fulfilling [sic] work"

0504
"meaningful work – work that fully engages our talents in something we believe in"

0505
"my Daemon … your Daemon"

0506
"my higher purpose and how I may [sic] manifest it more fully in my life"

0507
"my inner guide"

0508
"my mission in life"

0509
"my quest for meaning"

0510
"my real life work"

A musician must make music, an artist must paint, a poet must write, if he is to be ultimately at peace with himself. This need we may call self-actualization.

Abraham Maslow

0511
"my true self"

0512
"my true life purpose"

0513
"my true vocation"

0514
"my unique greatness, my gifts and talents, my life force"

0515
"my work for the benefit of other sentient beings"

0516
"native capacity"

0517
"native gifts"

0518
"natural [desire] to serve other people in some meaningful way"

0519
"natural competence"

0520
"natural strength areas, where you could become a superstar"

All the world's a stage
And all men and women merely players.
They have their exits and entrances;
Each man in his time plays many parts.

William Shakespeare

0521
"natural urge for growth and fulfillment"

0522
"new kinds of work that can defend our planet's well-being and thereby our own"

0523
"offer[ing] ourselves to the world [whereby] the world gives itself back to us"

0524
"one of our most valuable spiritual faculties"

0525
"[one's] existence as a human being"

0526
"one's higher self"

0527
"one's innermost source of power"

0528
"one's own core character"

0529
"one's own function in life"

0530
"[one's] own meaningful commitment to life with all of [one's] being"

There is no one who can take our place. Each of us weaves a strand in the web of creation. What we have to contribute is both unique and irreplaceable. … The entire world depends on our individual choices.

Duane Elgine

0531
"one's own nature"

0532
"one's personal dedication to a cause greater than oneself"

0533
"one's place in the universe"

0534
"one's potential best self"

0535
"one's soul finding its weight and measure"

0536
"one's specific vocation or mission in life to carry out a concrete assignment which demands fulfillment"

0537
"one's true self"

0538
"one's unique potentials"

0539
"oneness with the life process"

0540
"oneness with nature"

Empowerment might be thought of as a form of awakening to the reality that we are powerful; that we have unique skills and talents that can serve the world around us, and bring betterment to the planet; that we are basically good and can trust ourselves and one another; that we can tap our courage, inner strength, creativity and spontaneity to make a difference in the world ...

Willis Harman and John Hormann

0541
"opening our hearts to whatever it was that captured our imagination as children ... something that so occupied our thoughts that we felt foolish talking about it and yet found we could speak of nothing else ... what so filled us with curiosity and joy that words could not do justice to it ... [what had] been forgotten and buried ... what had to be sacrificed in order for us to fulfill the expectations of others and live in a reasonable adult world"

0542
"opportunity to return [our] unique gift to the community"

0543
"opportunities for inner growth"

0544
"our ability to invest psychic energy in the future"

0545
"our artfulness ... an integral part of ourselves ... a vitality, an impulse, a place of inner nourishment; it serves as a reminder that no matter what life brings us, we can always come back to the well"

0546
"[our] authentic work"

0547
"our authenticity"

0548
"our basic human urge to play a meaningful and respected role at work"

0549
"our basic inclinations"

0550
"our being able to contribute to the work of the universe"

Everybody needs a niche. All of us need to achieve a place, establish an identifiable role, make a recognized contribution … This means both that we must provide something significant or distinctive and that others must acknowledge it.

Robert Evans

0551
"our being, our ground, our depths, our inner selves"

0552
"our birthright … to live imaginative and original lives"

0553
"our calling for our spiritual existence … work that is more than a livelihood"

0554
"our callings, the wisdom of our true natures"

0555
"our capacity for connecting to the Great Work"

0556
"our capacity to do the unnatural, to transcend and hence transform our own nature"

0557
"our Center of Focus"

0558
"our continual search for meaning and direction in our lives"

0559
"our contribution [sic] to progress, to the divine task which … insures immortality"

0560
"our core"

You are you, unique, important to the universe, and you should assess your own worth instead of letting others do it for you.

Sanders G. Laurie and Melvin J. Tucker

0561
"our deeper inner purposes"

0562
"our deeper needs"

0563
"our deepest aspirations"

0564
"our deepest callings"

0565
"our deepest center"

0566
"our deepest contribution to the community"

0567
"our deepest desire and our true calling"

0568
"our deepest dimension – our essence – where we have a profound sense of who we are, where we came from, and where we are going"

0569
"our deepest longings"

0570
"our deepest personal urgencies"

There is only one YOU. Think about that. Your face and features, your voice, your style, your background, your characteristics and peculiarities, your abilities, your smile, your walk, your handshake, your manner of expression, your viewpoint … everything about you is found in only one individual since man first began – YOU. … Dig as deeply as you please in the ancient, dusty archives of Homo sapiens and you'll not find another YOU in the whole lot. And that, by the way, did not just happen; it was planned that way.

Charles R. Swindoll

0571
"our deepest rewards from work"

0572
"our deepest selves"

0573
"our deepest truth"

0574
"our desire to create a better world"

0575
"our endowments"

0576
"our essence"

0577
"our essential nature as humans"

0578
"our evolutionary imperative"

0579
"[our] existential anxieties"

0580
"our full potential as great souls that can ceaselessly create"

Go to work, and above all cooperate and don't hold back on one another or try to gain at the expense of another. Any success in such lopsidedness will be increasingly short-lived. These are the synergetic rules that evolution is employing and trying to make clear to us. They are not man-made laws. They are the infinitely accommodative laws of the universe.

R. Buckminster Fuller

0581
"our gifts to others' needs and their gifts to our needs"

0582
"[our] goals in life, [our] reasons for living, and [our] relation to the cosmos as a whole"

0583
"[our] great life work"

0584
"our great spiritual endowment"

0585
"our greater true selves"

0586
"our greatest abilities"

0587
"our healthiest impulse"

0588
"our heart's deep desires"

0589
"our higher nature"

0590
"our highest concept of life"

Each of us has an inner compass that helps us know where to go and what to do.

Gloria Steinem

0591
"our highest purpose"

0592
"our human participation in the dream of the Earth, the dream that is carried in its integrity not in any of Earth's cultural expressions but in the depths of our genetic coding"

0593
"our hungers"

0594
"our identity with the unity that lies within and beyond the diversity of all things"

0595
"[our] immutable essence [as humans]"

0596
"our inborn ability to keep learning new ways of interacting with the world"

0597
"our inborn urge"

0598
"[our] individuality"

0599
"[our] inherent purpose"

0600
"our inherent worth and the inherent worth in all"

Why has inner development, the basis of all success and happiness in life, the most fundamental aspect of our education, been neglected?

Jack Forem

0601
"our inmost selves"

0602
"our inner being"

0603
"our inner development"

0604
"our inner fire'

0605
"our inner guidance"

0606
"our inner imperative"

0607
"our inner life [and] the source of how we choose to act and to live"

0608
"our inner life, our state of mind, our character"

0609
"our inner nature"

0610
"our inner needs"

What do we teach our children in school?

We teach them that two and two make four
and that Paris is the capital of France.
When will we also teach them what they are?

We should say to each of them:
Do you know what you are? You are a marvel.
You are unique. In all of the world there is no
other child exactly like you. In the millions of
years that have passed, there has never been
a child like you. And look at your body – what
a wonder it is! Your legs, your arms, your
cunning fingers, the way you move! You may
become a Shakespeare, a Michelangelo, a
Beethoven. You have the capacity for
anything.

Yes, you are a marvel. And when you grow up, can
you then harm another who is, like you, a marvel?
You must cherish one another. We must all work --
to make this world worthy of its children.

Pablo Casals

0611

"our inner rhythms, which are part of the overarching rhythms of nature. By honoring these rhythms we bring greater peace to ourselves and our world"

0612

"our inner sense of direction"

0613

"our inner strength and greatness"

0614

"our inner voice ... the wisdom of the organism"

0615

"our inner wisdom"

0616

"our intimacy with the natural world"

0617

"our largest untapped natural resource – human potential"

0618

"our life's task"

0619

"our life-giving powers"

0620

"[our] most potent lever for change and [our] ultimate source of power"

That I am human
I have in common with all people;
That I see and hear
And eat and drink
I share with all animals.
But that I am I is exclusively mine,
And belongs to me
And nobody else,
To no other person
Nor to an angel nor to God,
Except inasmuch as I am one with God.

Meister Eckhart

0621
"our most unique roles, where we can have the greatest influence"

0622
"our most uniquely individual beliefs about what is important"

0623
"our mystery-filled, star-born nature"

0624
"our natural abilities"

0625
"our natural genius"

0626
"our natural inclinations"

0627
"our needs and motivations and the purpose we have given our lives"

0628
"our oneness with life"

0629
"our oneness with nature and with one another"

0630
"our own calling, our unique way of adding value to the planet"

What lies before us and what lies behind us are small matters compared to what lies within us. And when we bring what is within out into the world, miracles happen.

Henry David Thoreau

0631
"our own essential natures"

0632
"our own highest values"

0633
"our own inner music"

0634
"our own inner wisdom"

0635
"our own life direction"

0636
"[our] own particular skills and interests"

0637
"our own remarkable way of expressing our humanity"

0638
"our own stories"

0639
"our own truest voice"

0640
"our own unique potential, to achieve … 'self-actualization'"

By virtue of being born a human being, having a certain kind of body and nervous system (the hardware), and functioning in the general environment of spaceship Earth, a very wide variety of behaviors and experiences are potentially available to you. … But any individual human being will only develop a small fraction of his total human potentialities because he is born into a particular culture at a particular place and time, has certain parents, relatives, peers, and teachers, and has various random events happen to him. A culture can be looked at as the creation of a group of programmers [sic] who have (implicitly) agreed that certain human potentialities are beneficial and should be developed, and have set up a society, a system of interlocking relationships, to select these potentialities out of the total spectrum of human potentialities, to develop them, and to program them, to various degrees.

Charles T. Tart

0641
"our own unique potentials to become extraordinary in our own right"

0642
"our own uniqueness"

0643
"our own work and mission"

0644
"our part in the ever-evolving universe"

0645
"our part in the harmony of nature"

0646
"[our] part in the larger human community"

0647
"our participation in an inclusive oneness, a process much larger than ourselves"

0648
"our passionate fulfillment of soul purpose"

0649
"our personal participation in evolution, our duty"

0650
"our place in the life process"

The extraordinarily creative individual may simply be extraordinarily good at whatever skill is required to do a great job in a given domain. … [T]hese extraordinary skills will not be relevant to every problem the individual works on, which means there will be cases in which the "genius" may produce merely ordinary work.

Robert W. Weisberg

0651
"our primary source of guidance in the inherent tendencies of our genetic coding"

0652
"our purpose … to give ourselves to the world around us – including people, musical instruments, trees, and words – and through the attention we bring to them help them blaze to life"

0653
"our real names [which] only God knows"

0654
"our real nature"

0655
"our real purpose"

0656
"our real work … our real journey"

0657
"[our] reasons for living and what [we] might leave as legacy"

0658
"our reservoir of expertise … our wellspring of inspiration deeper than we can fully tap"

0659
"our rich inner, human core"

0660
"[our] right work"

Education, to justify itself, should enable a man to use the full potential of his body, mind, and spirit.

Maharishi Mahesh Yogi

0661
"[our] role in the integral functioning of the planet"

0662
"our selves"

0663
"our shining, life-giving completeness"

0664
"our singular place and connection within the whole"

0665
"our soul's awakening"

0666
"[our] special abilities"

0667
"our spiritual purpose for living"

0668
"our trails to blaze"

0669
"our true calling in life"

0670
"our true character and individuality"

Each of us has the capacity to become much more than we think we can be, if we choose to stop believing otherwise.

Willis Harman and Howard Rheingold

0671
"our true destiny"

0672
"our true, moral, rational and spiritual nature as a species

0673
"our true nature"

0674
"our true, unique selves"

0675
"our true vocations"

0676
"our true voice"

0677
"our truest self"

0678
"our ultimate human right"

0679
"our ultimate nature"

0680
"our unique differences"

The war furnished overwhelming proof that the rank and file can shine creatively when stirred by a patriotic urge.

Alex F. Osborn

0681
"our unique gifts"

0682
"our unique human endowment"

0683
"our uniquely human potential"

0684
"our unity with all there is in divine purpose"

0685
"our unlimited capacity for growth and change"

0686
"our unlimited potential"

0687
"our varied selves"

0688
"our vast potential and limitless possibility"

0689
"our vast, true nature"

0690
"our very being"

Nothing splendid has ever been achieved except by those who dared believe that something inside them was superior to circumstance.

Bruce Barton

0691
"our vocations and purpose in living"

0692
"our willed impulses"

0693
"[our] work … an expression of the Spirit at work in the world through us"

0694
"our worth as human beings"

0695
"participation in the act of God creating the cosmos. God creates the cosmos, we create the microcosmos, the 'human world'"

0696
"participating in the Great Work of the universe"

0697
"passionate fulfillment of soul purpose"

0698
"passionate longing to grow, to be"

0699
"peak experiences … moments when the glory of life, the beauty, perfection and unity of the cosmos are revealed to us, making all of life worthwhile"

0700
"penetrating into the deeper levels of who we are … know[ing] that those qualities being released from within us may prove to be our greatest strengths"

The only failure a man ought to fear is failure in cleaving to the purpose he sees to be best.

George Eliot

0701
"people's striving for a sense of wholeness or completeness"

0702
"perceiving hitherto unnoticed opportunity ... the 'what else is there that has not been recognized before'"

0703
"personal illumination"

0704
"personal mission in life"

0705
"personal perspective on the world"

0706
"personal search for challenging possibilities for action in daily life"

0707
"personal sense of destiny"

0708
"personal work [that] needs to be aligned with the Great Work"

0709
"pioneer[ing] uncharted paths"

0710
"playing a role in making the cosmic wheel go around"

It can be said flatly that the mere act of listening to wise statements and sound advice does little for anyone … no amount of information, whether of theory or fact, in itself improves insight and judgment or increases ability to act wisely under conditions of responsibility … We cannot effectively use the insight and knowledge of others; it must be our own knowledge and insight that we use … So far as responsible activity in the business world is concerned, it is clear that a fund of ready-made answers can be of little avail. Each situation is a new situation, requiring imaginative understanding as a prelude to sound judgment and action.

Charles Gragg

0711
"play[ing] your own music [which] if you don't do it yourself ... the world will be the poorer without it"

0712
"positive becoming and maturing"

0713
"possibilities of being ... possibilities of action"

0714
"possibilities that are a man's birthright"

0715
"potential that all people have [sic] that, with effort, can expand"

0716
"potentials I would otherwise not have realized"

0717
"potentialities inherent in every human existence"

0718
"potentialities inherent in the station of man, the full measure of his destiny on earth, the innate excellence of his reality"

0719
"potentialities which we had all the time but never used"

0720
"potentials all of us have that are in the process of manifesting themselves"

Half the difficulties of man lie in his desire to answer every question with yes or no.

Somerset Maugham

0721
"powerful forces that drive our behavior"

0722
"powers of the mind vastly superior to your rational powers"

0723
"psychic energy"

0724
"psychic imperative"

0725
"psychic life"

0726
"psychic meanings"

0727
"psycho-spiritual growth"

0728
"pure potentiality seeking expression from the unmanifest to the manifest"

0729
"purpose – a natural reason for being with [which] each of us was born [sic]"

0730
"purpose and significance you attach [sic] to your life"

Lack of willpower has caused more failure than lack of intelligence or ability.

Flower A. Newhouse

0731
"purpose … the engine that powers our lives"

0732
"purposeful unfolding of human potentialities toward goals"

0733
"pushing old boundaries, running up against the system in all its ferocious stubbornness"

0734
"questions that cry out from the depth of your soul"

0735
"reaching out to the world in loving service"

0736
"real success"

0737
"realizing one's ecological, wider or big Self"

0738
"rebirth[ing] the world in all of its detail again and again … nam[ing] the world and help[ing] other people recognize the grace, wisdom and wonder that have been present all along"

0739
"reinventing the human within the community of life systems"

0740
"resources buried in [your] inner self"

Born original, how comes it to pass that we die copies?

Edward Young

0741
"responsibilities we each have [sic] that influence where the world is heading"

0742
"reunion with all life"

0743
"Right Livelihood … work that is truly satisfying … [something we do] for the sake of the work itself … without any thought of pay"

0744
"seeing beyond ego to the larger pattern"

0745
"seeing what others cannot see"

0746
"seek[ing] not just our personal advantage [but] the collective well-being of all life"

0747
"self-discovery which is in reality an uncovering of something already present though unrecognized"

0748
"self-expression"

0749
"self-realization … realizing what we already are … finding [sic] greater inner resources and effortlessly living [sic] richer, more meaningful lives"

0750
"sense of oneness with other beings and … a desire to heal society"

People must recover the lost aspects of their personalities, lost under a pile of inhibitions, if they are to become integrated in any effective sense.

Rollo May

0751
"signs of the soul that lies hidden in the everyday and commonplace"

0752
"some insight, some perspective that is struggling to be born"

0753
"some meaning and purpose worth living for"

0754
"some purpose or mission in life that all of us have to find [sic] which will confer upon us a sense of personal distinction and worth"

0755
"some special ability or keen interest that can be developed, whether it is a knack for doing mechanical things, for building things, or for working well with other people"

0756
"something, a question perhaps or a curiosity, one not yet fully formed, but one whose nature is so compelling that we are drawn to it like a gravity pull"

0757
"something (an aim, a passion, an interest, a problem, an idea) [that] attracts us enough to move us to action on its behalf and is important enough so that focusing on it directs our activities and provides our lives with a sense of meaning"

0758
"something basic in human nature"

0759
"something burning inside you [that] will come out in action"

0760
"something critical to us all"

The great men who stand out in history have been partly benefactors of mankind and partly quite the reverse ... But all these men, good and bad alike, had a quality which I should not like to see disappear from the world -- a quality of energy and personal initiative, of independence of mind, and of imaginative vision.

Bertrand Russell

0761
"something deep within us [that] will always remain uneasy until we discover and live what we were born to do"

0762
"something deeper that we can call upon for help when we are discouraged [sic] … a part of ourselves that cannot be defeated"

0763
"something encoded in your cells that you must do, something that is your basic reason for being on the planet"

0764
"something for the sake of which to live and even to die"

0765
"something fundamental about yourself"

0766
"something fundamentally human"

0767
"something greater than the concerns that fill our days"

0768
"something I really want to do … something I enjoy doing … something I am likely to enjoy doing in the foreseeable future … something I will be able to live with myself if I accomplish it"

0769
"something inside me which will not permit me to accept [the] conclusion … that life has no meaning"

0770
"something limitless and unbounded"

The principal goal of education is to create men and women who are capable of doing new things, not simply of repeating what other generations have done. … men and women who are creative, inventive discoverers. The second goal of education is to form minds which can be critical, can verify and not accept everything they are offered.

Jean Piaget

0771
"something meaningful to accomplish each day that you can't wait to get started on it"

0772
"something precious in people"

0773
"something [that] is continually speaking within us"

0774
"something that only we can do. That gift [that] comes to us so naturally that often we don't know we are doing it at all"

0775
"something that outstanding executives have in common with gifted military commanders, brilliant political leaders, great artists"

0776
"something that reaches inside us and pulls out our best efforts"

0777
"something that satisfies my longing as nothing else can do"

0778
"something that transcends our own lives and taps the best energies within us"

0779
"something that we are … crystallized in the course of the evolution of our species … founded on our biological past and rooted in our biological depth … ultimately anchored in our biological heritage"

0780
"something that you can do better than anyone else in the whole world"

It takes courage to be creative. Just as soon as you have a new idea, you are a minority of one.

E. Paul Torrance

0781
"something that we are"

0782
"something truly unprecedented"

0783
"something unique, different, unlike anything else that ever was or ever shall be, the original Thinker thinking a new manifestation"

0784
"something unique [that] everyone is called to be and to do"

0785
"something valuable [that] each of us has to offer the world"

0786
"something we all have [sic] to contribute to the healing of the whole"

0787
"something we are being 'called' to, by our muse, by an inner voice, by a higher presence, by something greater than us"

0788
"something we cannot penetrate … our perceptions of the profoundest reason and the most radiant beauty"

0789
"something we genuinely find interesting; yet it is a sense of being more ourselves"

0790
"something you do because you must do it. You want to do it, you love doing it, you're excited when you do it. And you'd do it even if you were paid nothing beyond food and the basics. You do it because it's your life"

The greatest loss in the world is loss of human potential.

Leo Buscaglia

0791
"something you find interesting, for a reason hard to explain. It is hard to explain because you have never read it on a page. You were made and set here to give voice to this, your own astonishment"

0792
"soul work"

0793
"soul-deep meaning"

0794
"soul-purpose"

0795
"special talents we all possess [sic], a unique ability to do the work we were made for"

0796
"specific vocation or mission in life … a concrete assignment that demands fulfillment [and that] everyone must carry out"

0797
"state of higher being"

0798
"staying in touch with your inner self, with your higher self, with your God-like self or soul"

0799
"stored-up reserves of energy that are ordinarily not called upon – deeper and deeper strata of exploitable material, ready for use by anyone who probes so deep"

0800
"strengths and skills of your soul [that] want to be used"

The goal of self-esteem, and the demands of many humans, make it clear that the very questions about humanness and human nature and human potential are the most important questions for schools and education today.

John Vasconcellos

0801
"striving to be ourselves in the particular area that makes us distinctive and outstanding"

0802
"striving toward meaningful goals – goals that relate the individual to a larger context of purposes"

0803
"submitting [yourself] to something [you] consider greater than [yourself]"

0804
"tak[ing] an inner issue – one that comes by listening to our own images – and work[ing] on it, constructing a form for it, squeezing it, shaking it, pruning it, coloring it, and dreaming on it, and then … offer[ing] our work to the community at large"

0805
"talents and abilities [with which] every one of us is specially equipped that give us the potential to make a unique contribution to the world"

0806
"that core, that essence that I call myself, my spirit [and that] I take with me from one context to another"

0807
"that deep but familiar longing that speaks of what we truly want"

0808
"that deep place of divine activity"

0809
"that 'God' within each of us: the higher self"

0810
"that heartfelt and poetic feeling [that] could come only from inside of me"

Beginning with school, if not before, an individual is systematically stripped of his imagination, his creativity, his heritage, his dreams and his personal uniqueness, in order to fit him into a productive unit in a mass technological society ... As the individual is drawn into the meritocracy, his working life is split from his home life, and both suffer from a lack of wholeness. Eventually, people virtually become their professions, roles, or occupations and are thenceforth strangers to themselves.

Charles Reich

0811
“that essential mystery at the heart of each human life”

0812
“that feeling which our nine-to-five jobs may not be giving us, of using our skills, making a difference, and being appreciated”

0813
“that ‘fire that burns within’ that impels people to keep pushing, to never be satisfied, and to always search for improvement”

0814
“that force which directs all our actions, which is the source of all our delights and all our pursuits”

0815
“that inner wealth we have at our core”

0816
“that inner wellspring of wisdom”

0817
“that interior location where the real you lives … where your stories happen”

0818
“that interior place where spiritual life forms the rest of life”

0819
“that invisible mystery at the center of every life that speaks to the fundamental question ‘What is it, in my heart, that I must do, be, and have? And why?’”

0820
“that moment [when] the larger universe, of which we have always been a part but often ignored, has our full attention”

It is a sad fact that in the modern world most people never find their life's purpose. Some people who fail to do so are very successful by worldly standards. They have money, power, and prestige, but they aren't really happy. Something deep inside them is dissatisfied and restless. They may try to ignore or hide this feeling, but often that leads only to illness.

Mark Thurston

0821

"that natural instinct that propels us toward creation, choice, liberation and change"

0822

"that need which if fulfilled first, then everything else will follow"

0823

"that profound interaction with the universe"

0824

"that quiet inner voice that would teach us of true north principles and our own degree of congruency with them"

0825

"that self which one truly is"

0826

"that sense of caring for human salvation on earth"

0827

"that sense of inner meaning ... that sense of personal significance that [fills] my days and [drives] me from within"

0828

"that spark of life [that] all people have"

0829

"that spiritual wholeness which exists at the center of every person's being"

0830

"that underground river that will always bring forth new and different ideas each time"

We have abundant resources that remain unused. … One can find significance and meaning close at hand. … The creative man realizes that anything as vast as universal peace or equal rights for all mankind begins in small places close to his home.

Harvey Seifert

0831
"that which continuously unfolds around and within us"

0832
"that which gives purpose to my life and a reason to live"

0833
"that which is uniquely [yourself]"

0834
"that which makes human life meaningful and fulfilling"

0835
"that which only you can do"

0836
"that which sets humans apart from other creatures"

0837
"that which we most essentially are"

0838
"that which you really love to do"

0839
"that within me which is completely conscious of its unity with good, of its oneness with all the power there is, all the presence there is, and all the life there is"

0840
"that within me which understands the Truth, which completely accepts It, which remembers freedom, expresses freedom, and anticipates freedom"

Unfortunately, the vast majority of our human brothers and sisters do not look very much like the fully alive human being … self-actualizing or fully functioning. [M]ost of the others exist without really living. By common estimation, [sic] most people realize only about ten percent of their life-potential. They see only ten percent of the world's beauty and hear only ten percent of the music and poetry of the universe. They are alive to only ten percent of the deep and rich feelings possible to human beings. They stumble along the path of an unreflective life in an unexamined world. They survive with only a shriveled capacity for giving and receiving love.

John Powell

0841
"the abilities you have that make you a unique person"

0842
"the ability to see beyond our present reality, to create, to invent what does not yet exist"

0843
"the … active … determining force in [your] own life"

0844
"the active spontaneous core of [oneself]"

0845
"the actualization of a new idea or vision"

0846
"the actualization of potentials inherent in all of us"

0847
"the actualization of what [one] potentially is"

0848
"the actualizing tendency [that] is present in all living organisms"

0849
"the aim and purpose of human life"

0850
"the answers to our own being, our own identity"

In education we tend to turn out conformists, stereotypes ... rather than freely creative and original thinkers.

In our leisure time activities, passive entertainment and regimented group action are overwhelmingly predominant while creative action are much less in evidence.

In the sciences, there is an ample supply of technicians, but the number who can creatively formulate fruitful hypotheses and theories is small indeed.

In industry, creation is reserved for the few ... while for the many life is devoid of original or creative endeavor.

In individual and family life the same picture holds true. In the clothes we wear, the food we eat, the books we read, and the ideas we hold, there is a strong tendency toward conformity, toward stereotypy. To be original, or different, is felt to be dangerous.

Carl R. Rogers

0851
"the appropriate direction for [each person's] growth"

0852
"the art of being"

0853
"the authentic wellsprings that have fertilized our thought and shaped our consciousness"

0854
"the authentically human"

0855
"the basic impulse informing all our past history"

0856
"the basic personhood that we all have"

0857
"the basic plot of my story"

0858
"the basis of all success and happiness in life"

0859
"the basis of everything we do"

0860
"the best human qualities"

Everyone knows that on any given day there are energies slumbering in him which the incitements of that day do not call forth. Compared with what we ought to be, we are only half awake. Our fires are damped, our drafts are checked. We are making use of only a small part of our possible mental and physical resources.

William James

0861
"the best in man"

0862
"the best in man's nature [and] also the best hope for his future survival"

0863
"the best of what it is to be human"

0864
"the best or ultimate qualities for human development"

0865
"the best that is [sic] in us"

0866
"the biggest possible truth of what it means to be human and alive now"

0867
"the biogenetic force we see expressed in every living organism"

0868
"the birthright of our children"

0869
"the blithe spirit inside [each of us] who keeps trying to come out and play"

0870
"the blossoming of our real nature"

Only a small proportion of the population today understands that they have the potential to control their future, to make significant decisions about the sort of world they want for themselves, their family, and their community. The rest of society feels helpless to affect their universe. They feel they are locked, without options, into a job/income/consumption pattern.

Robert Theobald

0871
"the 'blueprints' that give direction to the course of a biography"

0872
"the body of mankind integrated with the essence of all earth; the collective mind reaching beyond into a universe of infinite potential"

0873
"the buried longings of our lives that are always urging to be satisfied"

0874
"the call of [our] souls"

0875
"the call of the heart"

0876
"the call that beckons us to search"

0877
"[the] call to our imaginative life"

0878
"the call to service"

0879
"the call within each of us, but to which most of us have been unable to respond"

0880
"the capability 'to be' that is not as yet in being"

It is nothing short of a miracle that the modern methods of instruction have not yet entirely strangled the holy curiosity of inquiry; for this delicate little plant, aside from stimulation, stands mainly in need of freedom; without this it goes to wreck and ruin without fail. It is a very grave mistake to think that the enjoyment of seeing and searching can be promoted by means of coercion and a sense of duty.

Albert Einstein

0881
“the capability we all have [sic] to function on a much higher (or deeper) level than we ordinarily do”

0882
“the capacity for continuous self-renewal”

0883
“[the] capacity for self renewal”

0884
“the capacity to be [oneself], to see the world in [one’s] own unique and independent fashion”

0885
“the capacity to be original, to express yourself as yourself”

0886
“the capacity to find greatness in the everyday”

0887
“the capacity to go beyond the individual self and find meaning and purpose in something greater than oneself”

0888
“the capacity to live more fully”

0889
“the capacity to make new combinations”

0890
“the capacity to perceive and conceive one’s world, to reach out toward it to form and re-form it”

Considering man's hostility to change and innovation ... it is astonishing that so much of creative and imaginative genius has contrived to leave its impress on the human race. Yet who can doubt that more, habited in weak bodies, blasted early by ignorance and cruelty and superstition, has perished with no record. In our comparatively low civilization a little is done under favorable circumstances to salvage great talent. Yet how pitifully meager is our salvage and how great the waste! We know that this is so. A more civilized time than ours will strive to develop this, the greatest of all natural resources.

Carl H. Grabo

0891
"the capacity to rise above biological, psychological, or sociological conditions, to grow beyond them"

0892
"the center and what is highest in humanity"

0893
"the center of our being"

0894
"the center of our life and origin of our thinking and acting"

0895
"the center of one's self"

0896
"the center of the vitality of a culture – its heart and soul"

0897
"the center of what is highest in humanity"

0898
"the center point of our life"

0899
"the center, which is yours and that of all humanity"

0900
"the central core of the person"

A frog if put in cold water will not bestir itself if that water is heated up slowly and gradually and will in the end let itself be boiled alive, too comfortable with continuity to realize that continuous change at some point may become intolerable and demand a change in behavior. If we want to avoid the fate of … the boiling frog we must learn to look for and embrace discontinuous change.

Charles Handy

0901
"the central meaning of our lives"

0902
"the central needs of people"

0903
"the central source of meaning in our lives"

0904
"the chi energies [that] circulate throughout all existence"

0905
"the chief characteristic of a complex self"

0906
"the chief purpose of life"

0907
"the child's need to be able to say 'I am somebody'"

0908
"the code of the soul"

0909
"the compelling necessity which the individual feels to search for and become himself"

0910
"the conditions for a specific line of development [that] have yet to achieve fruition"

We don't live up to the potential for excellence that is the birthright of every person. … If society hopes to achieve renewal, it will have to be a hospitable environment for creative men and women.

John W. Gardner

0911
"the constant radiation of what man really is, not what he pretends to be"

0912
"the constructive initiative that gives significance to life"

0913
"the continuing work of life"

0914
"the cooperative side of human nature"

0915
"the core heart values that make up a world worth living in"

0916
"the core of us"

0917
"the core, the essence of one's being"

0918
"the cosmos' work"

0919
"the courage to be individual, to speak with one's own voice"

0920
"the courage to be which unites the courage to be as a part … and the courage to be as oneself by transcending both"

Thousands of geniuses live and die undiscovered – either by themselves or by others.

Mark Twain

0921
"the courage to do what seems to [us] significant in [our] lives"

0922
"the Creator's divine gifts to you"

0923
"the daimon's urgings"

0924
"the deep and lasting happiness that we all seek"

0925
"the deep calling to make a contribution ... to make a positive difference with our lives"

0926
"the deep center"

0927
"the deep core of who we are and what we are about"

0928
"the deep inner core of personal empowerment"

0929
"the deep inner needs of our nature"

0930
"the deep place from which life flows"

The greatest waste of our natural resources is the number of people who never achieve their potential.

Charles Swindoll

0931
“the deep source of life”

0932
“the deeper inner purposes of our hearts”

0933
“the deeper needs of the soul”

0934
“the deeper or spiritual side of [our] nature”

0935
“the deeper source for our work”

0936
“the deeper springs of action in persons”

0937
“the deepest and best within you”

0938
“the deepest and most nourishing cisterns of our inner life”

0939
“the deepest and most powerful current [sic] of human consciousness”

0940
“the deepest concern [sic] of humanity throughout the ages”

The disease of civilization is not so much the material poverty of the many as the decay of the spirit of freedom and self-confidence.

G. D. H. Cole and W. Mellor

0941
"the deepest desire we all share"

0942
"the deepest human experience"

0943
"the deepest longings of our hearts"

0944
"the deepest of human needs"

0945
"the deepest part of [our] heart and soul [that] brings out the best and subordinates the rest"

0946
"the deepest parts of [our] beings"

0947
"the deepest purpose for which [each of us] was born"

0948
"the deepest responsibility of each of us … to become more fully who we are"

0949
"the deepest urge in human nature"

0950
"the deepest, widest questions of our being"

If people feel that they cannot effect change, they are more likely to retreat into their isolated worlds. They are also more likely to look for pleasure in the technological conveniences and material products the society of plentitude provides for them – that is, people end up being pacified and addicted to the very forces that rob them of an authentic sense of happiness and accomplishment. No wonder we are increasingly depressed.

Thomas Lombardo and Jonathan Richter

0951
"the deepest yearning of every soul"

0952
"the defiant power of the human spirit"

0953
"the defining characyersitics of humanness, or personhood"

0954
"the desire for meaning and purpose"

0955
"the desire to be great"

0956
"the desire to be important"

0957
"the desire to be someone, to have status, to belong, to act, to contribute and to grow"

0958
"[the] desire to be what we are"

0959
"the desire to contribute, to make a positive difference with our lives"

0960
"the development of human beings to their fullest expression"

Dissatisfaction, apathy, boredom, lack of joy and happiness, a sense of futility and a vague feeling that life is meaningless, are the unavoidable result s of [alienated work].

Erich Fromm

0961
"the diamond ... inside us, waiting to be discovered, shaped, and polished"

0962
"the dignity of the child's being ... the right to be the kind of child he is"

0963
"the directional trend which is evident in all organic and human life – the urge to expand, extend, develop, mature – the tendency to express and activate all the capacities of the organism, to the extent that such activation enhances the organism or the self"

0964
"the divine child in us all"

0965
"the divine, eternal, and changeless you"

0966
"the divine nature within ourselves"

0967
"the divine spark [that] is in every man"

0968
"the divine touch in the individual"

0969
"the dominant force in your life"

0970
"the dominant necessity of human nature"

A good formula for disaster is to attempt to make decisions affecting the future of a person, a society, or the planet, based on a perception of reality that isn't true. Many persons in recent years have been shocked at realizing that is precisely what modern society has been attempting to do.

Willis Harman and John Hormann

0971
"the drive for progress [that] pushes from within for continuous change and forward movement"

0972
"the drive … to beat the odds, achieve great things, and become something truly extraordinary"

0973
"the drive to go further, to do better, to create new possibilities"

0974
"the duties appointed for [man] by his world"

0975
"the dynamic forces needed to create the future"

0976
"the dynamics that lie behind what you feel, what you perceive, what you value, and how you act"

0977
"the Earth … calling all of us to take a critical look at the work we do and the work we are not doing. This calling constitutes the new vocations of our generation, the new 'roles' we must play"

0978
"the end and purpose of [humanity's] being"

0979
"the end of human purposeful behavior"

0980
"the endless talents buried within us"

What is the true meaning of life? … What is the best plan for a national economy? What is the most fundamental value against which everything else can be measured? Too few … thinkers look seriously at such questions any more. That may be more of what is wrong with us than we realize.

Win Wenger

0981
"the endlessly recombining elements that make up works of fiction [poetry, art, music, science, etc.]"

0982
"the endowments which distinguish the human race from all other forms of life"

0983
"the enduring aspects of human life"

0984
"the energy and wisdom we bring to every role in our lives"

0985
"the energy out of which our actions spring and the true 0986

0986
"the ennobling purposes for which humanity was called into being"

0987
"the essence of being and aliveness"

0988
"the essence of each person"

0989
"the essence of existence"

0990
"the essence of human nature"

Most people have been trained to deny the freedom to find out who they really are. Not only have they failed to cultivate their creative potentials as persons, but are unaware that they even have such potential. Their education has oppressed them and made them slaves to conformist expectations. This is disastrous kind of education for people, especially for leaders who must not only find their own way like the rest of us, but guide us as we all face increasing obsolescence.

Reuel L. Howe

0991
“the essence of life”

0992
“the essence of what makes us human”

0993
“the essence of the work of the universe”

0994
“the essence of what life is all about”

0995
“the essence of who we truly are”

0996
“the essence of who you are”

0997
“the essence of why we have been placed here on this Earth”

0998
“the essential core [of a person]”

0999
“the essential impulse, without which nothing can be done”

1000
“the essential meaning of [our] life”

One of our problems is that very few of us have developed any distinctive personal life. Everything about us seems secondhand, even our emotions. In many cases we have to rely on secondhand information in order to live. ... There has to be a personal word, a unique confrontation, if I am to come alive.

Alan Jones

1001
"the essential motivating factor in all life"

1002
"the essential nature of man"

1003
"the essential we embody"

1004
"the eternal essence of [our] being"

1005
"the evolutionary imperative at the heart of life itself"

1006
"the evolutionary vigour of mankind"

1007
"the experience of fullness of life"

1008
"the expression of the self within that gives life meaning – creates the world, in effect, for the [sic] person"

1009
"the feature of personality that is most outstanding – its manifest uniqueness of organization"

1010
"the feeling of being able to put [your] hidden talents to use"

We need to understand that the competitive model of the last two centuries — striving against others, trying to get to the top of the heap whatever the cost — is no longer feasible or desirable. The persistence of this model is now the prime reason why we cannot develop our own lives in sensible, valuable ways.

Robert Theobald

1011
"the feeling of having done something meaningful with [one's] life"

1012
"the feeling that [one] is responsible to life for something, however grim [one's] circumstance might be"

1013
"the feelings that there is a reason my unique person is here and that there are things I must attend to beyond the daily round and that give the daily round its reason"

1014
"the final ingredient which enables us to say 'I have lived and my life mattered'"

1015
"the finest and most enduring qualities we are aware of"

1016
"the fire inspiring us with the joy of action and the love of life"

1017
"the fire of compassion and love that [is] burning in the very center of [our] beings, inspiring [us] to follow [our] hearts"

1018
"the fire within"

1019
"the first, foremost, and last essence of the human species"

1020
"the flame that burns within us"

The person resides in being, not in having.

Paul Tournier

1021
"the flow experience … memorable moments [of] acting spontaneously, as if carried away by the tides of a current"

1022
"the flourishing of infinite diversity"

1023
"the … force beneath all existence"

1024
"the force field of your being"

1025
"the force that drives evolution"

1026
"the forces that drive you"

1027
"the foundations of one's sense of personal worth"

1028
"the fountainhead of the human experience"

1029
"the freedom to be"

1030
"the fulfillment of life"

Because there are many forces working to inhibit creativity, we must consciously try to neutralize them ...

Mike Woodcock and Dave Francis

1031
"the fulfillment of that which is specifically human in us"

1032
"the full use of one's powers and talents"

1033
"the fullest realization of human possibilities"

1034
"the fullness of who you are"

1035
"the fundamental and all-embracing obligation imposed upon man by the Creator"

1036
"the fundamental and all-important issue in each life"

1037
"the fundamental nature of human beings"

1038
"the fundamental significance of life"

1039
"the generative forces of life"

1040
"the generative impulse and the primary purpose underlying the whole of creation"

Ever more people today have the means to live but not the meaning to live for.

Victor Frankl

1041
"the genetically coded mystery of life"

1042
"the genius within"

1043
"the Glory of God that is within us. … not just in some of us, [but] in everyone"

1044
"the goal of life"

1045
"the goal the individual most wishes to achieve, the end which he knowingly and unknowingly pursues"

1046
"the gods or goddesses in embryo that are contained within us seek[ing] to be fully materialized"

1047
"the governing principle of the universe"

1048
"the great capacity for imagination with which we all have been endowed"

1049
"the great key to life"

1050
"the Great Work of the universe [that] we must join [sic]"

Most of us go to our graves with our music still inside.

Oliver Wendell Holmes, Jr.

1051
"the great things you feel you ought to be doing"

1052
"the greatest and final aim of human existence"

1053
"the greatest conquest for man … explor[ing] the 'inner space' of ourselves"

1054
"the greatest of all natural resources"

1055
"the greatest potential for goodness"

1056
"[the] greatest resource [of] any organization, institution, community, society, nation, or civilization"

1057
"the greatness in people … in every human spirit"

1058
"the greatness that is inherent in all of us"

1059
"the ground of a true life"

1060
"the ground of any well-lived life"

Genius, that amazing gift from the Creative Source, and talent should be developed in the child not only for the sake of the individual but even more for the sake of society itself. For creativeness brings scientific invention. It bestows the light of art and beauty to brighten the all too somber horizons of humanity.

Stanwood Cobb

1061
"the guidance of the higher self"

1062
"the guiding principle of a healthy person's life"

1063
"the healthiest and highest expression of human nature"

1064
"the heart of our lives, our soul, our substance"

1065
"the heart of our spiritual journey"

1066
"the heart of who you are"

1067
"the heart, the soul, and the innermost core of our being"

1068
"the 'heart-work' of releasing all the imprisoned images within us, images that, because we were repressing them, we never really knew"

1069
"the heroes within"

1070
"the hidden sources of our personality"

Everyone has talent. What is rare is the courage to follow the talent to the dark place where it leads.

Erica Jong

1071
“the high destiny of the individual, to serve rather than to rule”

1072
“the high meaning of existence”

1073
“the higher part of a man’s spirit, that which is separated from the human element and is capable ... of becoming one with the universal spirit”

1074
“the higher purpose of your life”

1075
“the highest aims of social or individual life”

1076
“the highest cause of the whole universe”

1077
“the highest destiny of man”

1078
“the highest experience”

1079
“the highest expression of human nature”

1080
“the highest expression of love”

No man can reveal to you aught but that which already lies half asleep in the dawning of your knowledge.

The teacher who walks in the shadow of the temple, among his followers, gives not of his wisdom but rather of his faith and lovingness.

If he is indeed wise he does not bid you enter the house of his wisdom, but rather leads you to the threshold of your own mind.

The astronomer may speak to you of his understanding of space, but he cannot give you his understanding.

The musician may sing to you the rhythm which is in all space, but he cannot give you the ear which arrests the rhythm nor the voice which echoes it.

And he who is versed in the science of numbers can tell of the regions of weight and measure, but he cannot conduct you thither …

Khalil Gibran

1081
"the highest goal of human life – fulfillment"

1082
"the highest laws of life"

1083
"the highest motivator"

1084
"the highest of all [human] values"

1085
"the highest principles for our aspirations"

1086
"the highest truth"

1087
"the human ability to see infinite possibilities in situations"

1088
"the human energies needed to assist in shaping a desirable future"

1089
"the human need for far more than material well-being alone"

1090
"the images in us that yearn to be born"

And so we find another kind of resistance, a denying of our best side, of our talents, of our finest impulses, of our highest potentials, of our creativeness. In brief this is the struggle against our own greatness, the fear of hubris.

Abraham H. Maslow

1091
"the immortality to which we aspire"

1092
"the impelling life force which manifests itself in the evolutionary process through creation of new forms and new relationships in the universe"

1093
"the implorings of personal evolution"

1094
"the importance of our lives"

1095
"the impulse to fulfillment"

1096
"the impulse to know and live your own calling"

1097
"the impulse which is the very essence of human dignity"

1098
"the incommunicable singularity of being which each of us possesses"

1099
"the individual identity of each human person"

1100
"the individual's [sic] … own purpose and meaning in life"

Your ultimate goal in life is to become your best self. … Most people have a secret prejudice against their own strengths, talents, and greatness. ... Perhaps it is easier to believe we have little potential than to admit our talents. In that way, we avoid the jealousies and demands of others ... stave off [our] colleagues' or friends' resentment and hostility.

Marsha Sinetar

1101
"the individual's coming to terms with himself and his life through what he is and does"

1102
"the individual's unique value"

1103
"the ineffable mystery of what it means to be alive"

1104
"the Infinite in everyone"

1105
"the infinite intelligence resident in the subconscious mind"

1106
"the inherent capacity to see beyond the limits of our present condition and transcend them"

1107
"the inherent possibilities of human development"

1108
"the inherent powers of passion for living that dwells in all of us"

1109
"the inherent wisdom of the mind and the body"

1110
"the innate goodness of man [who is] organized in such a manner from birth as to need to continue to grow and develop in his potentialities for goodness"

In the pursuit of the fullness of human life, everything depends on [our] frame of reference, [our] habitual outlook, [the] basic vision which [we] have of [ourselves], others, life, the world … All change in the quality of a person's life must grow out of a change in his or her vision. There can be no real and permanent change unless this vision is changed.

John Powell

1111
"the innate human desire for accomplishment and achievement"

1112
"the innate nature of man"

1113
"the inner capacity of all employees to contribute to the benefit of the organization"

1114
"the inner compulsion to be all that one ought to be"

1115
"the inner field of being"

1116
"the inner growth of the human being"

1117
"the inner guide"

1118
"the inner nature of man"

1119
"the inner needs of our species … the inner needs of our communities as well"

1120
"the inner potential in every one"

The reason for the slow progress of the world seems to lie in a single fact. Every man is born under the yoke, and grows up beneath the oppressions of his age.

John Jay Chapman

1121
"the inner self"

1122
"the inner spirit"

1123
"the inner wealth of humanity [that] is boundless"

1124
"the inner work of our species that has been so long neglected in our industrial work world"

1125
"the innocent child who is always alive within each of us – who sees no obstacles, no problems or negativity; who doesn't believe in words like can't and impossible, who is not blocked by hurtful experiences of the past"

1126
"the insight with which the scientist tries to see into nature"

1127
"the instinctive … part of our nature, the one that waits
patiently for the world to be a place of love … destined to meet
many bullies on the corner, including that part of ourselves that
would rather be ruled by fear than let this love be seen"

1128
"the intelligence at the core of every human being to grow and develop toward a very definite end, or goal"

1129
"the intrinsic powers of men"

1130
"the intrinsic value and destiny of every individual"

The idea of an education which will develop all man's natural gifts is certainly a true one. … Under the present system of education, man does not fully attain the object of his being.

Immanuel Kant

1131
"the invisible conductor of the orchestra of life"

1132
"the invisible divine you"

1133
"the invisible force behind the body … behind the mind"

1134
"the invisible, intangible you"

1135
"the invisible self that is you"

1136
"the invisible, mysterious, unfathomable depths of a person"

1137
"the invisibles in everyone's life"

1138
"the inward courage of Tao … to affirm … the more humane, just, and harmonious world to which we may one day hope to evolve"

1139
"the irresistible need to explore"

1140
"the journeys on which our growth is predicated"

Our greatest mistake is to neglect the cultivation of those virtues a person has, and try to exact from each person virtues he does not possess.

Hadrian

1141
"the key paths by which we learn and relate deeply to reality"

1142
"the key to progress in all facets of living"

1143
"the key to you"

1144
"the kind of self that leads to a complex and harmonious evolution"

1145
"the knowledge that nature has already given you"

1146
"the last inner freedom [that] cannot be lost … this spiritual freedom which cannot be taken away – that makes life meaningful and purposeful"

1147
"the law of one's own being. Follow it, and it means fulfillment; disregard it, and it means disaster"

1148
"the laws of nature"

1149
"the laws of our own nature [which] carry us to fulfillment"

1150
"the leader within"

It is not human nature we should accuse but the … conventions that pervert it.

Denis Diderot

1151

"the level of cosmic consciousness at which one identifies with the entire universe ... where one finds one's supreme identity ... conscious awareness ... in which all boundaries and dualisms have been transcended and all individuality dissolves into universal, undifferentiated oneness"

1152

"the life and the intelligence within me that [sic] is some part of the Universal Spirit"

1153

"the life force and spirit that every human being and all life share"

1154

"the life force that flows through each person"

1155

"the life principle in you"

1156

"the life-force of Mankind"

1157

"the life-force within every individual [that is constantly pressing to be developed and expressed]"

1158

"the light within us"

1159

"the limitless field of possibilities"

1160

"the limitless possibilities residing latent in citizens' minds"

The job today is to realize the existence of the vast reservoir of creative potential in our people that lies latent and dormant, that needs release, that must be put to work, and should be developed further.

Leo B. Moore

1161
"the link between our inner work and the outer work that society requires of us ... the threshold through which our non-action leads to actions of beautification, celebration, and healing in the world"

1162
"the long-term direction of our life"

1163
"the lots our souls selected"

1164
"the mainspring of human progress"

1165
"the mainspring of life"

1166
"the mainsprings of a society's [sic] dynamism and talent and imagination"

1167
"[the] many ways in each of our communities that ... allow us to act with fresh ideas and vision and care and love"

1168
"the meaning and purpose of human life ... our place in the world ... our responsibilities to ourselves and others"

1169
"the meaning of human existence as well as ... man's search for such a meaning"

1170
"the meaning of life that makes people thirst for health and longevity"

The contemporary view posits that the correlation between intelligence and high socio-economic class is probably not due to genetic selection but rather to social conditioning ... If this is so (and it seems reasonable to suppose that it probably is), [sic] then the division of the curriculum according to the 'innate' capacity of the children to acquire knowledge is no longer an acceptable basis for classification.

John Vaizey

1171
"the meaning of one's life"

1172
"the mega-goal of personality … our need to maintain and enhance our self-worth … [to] view ourselves and be viewed by others as having worth and value as a person"

1173
"the mind, motivated by its own natural tendency to move in the direction of the infinite – that is, toward ever-increasing happiness and satisfaction"

1174
"the mind wandering … in search of fulfillment"

1175
"the most common and the most powerful motivation"

1176
"the most crucial of our needs"

1177
"the most fundamental aspect of the human"

1178
"[the] most fundamental human desires … the longing for transcendence and unity"

1179
"the most fundamental value against which everything else can be measured"

1180
"the most important experience that a soul can have in material life"

For the first time in man's life on earth, he is being asked to refrain from doing what he can do; he is being asked to restrain his economic and technological advancement, or at least to direct it differently from before; he is being asked by all the future generations of the earth to share his good fortune with the unfortunate -- not in a spirit of charity, but in a spirit of necessity. He is being asked to concentrate now on the organic growth of the total world system. Can he, in good conscience, say no?

The Club of Rome

1181
"the most important or powerful determinant [sic] of behavior"

1182
"the most important question [sic] of your life"

1183
"the most important thing to do in and with life"

1184
"the most precious parts of myself"

1185
"the most prized – and least understood – human trait"

1186
"the most profound question asked [of us] by life … the question of significance and meaning"

1187
"the most significant dimension of man that distinguishes him from all other beings"

1188
"the most thoroughly pervasive and peculiarly human trait of all"

1189
"the most valuable human quality"

1190
"the motivations that drive humankind forward"

Fulfillment means the realization of human potentials for existence as a biological and sociocultural being. … Self-fulfillment … is the end of human purposeful behavior. It is the actualization of potentials inherent in all of us.

Ervin Laszlo

1191
"the motive energy that impels all our actions"

1192
"the motive force behind all human endeavor"

1193
"the motive to realize one's full potential … the organism's master motive, the only real motive"

1194
"the music that waits inside you and yearns to be played"

1195
"the music within [each of us]"

1196
"the mysterious power behind some of our most ordinary mental activities"

1197
"the mysterious power of [our] own Being, which mediates between [us] and the mysterious power of the world's Being"

1198
"the mysterious unseen will … a regulator … a directing thought … the force which we cannot see"

1199
"the mystery of whatever it is that represents greatness in our own lives"

1200
"the nagging hunger for meaning"

We all must take responsibility for the world we share.

Clark W. Bullard

1201
"thc natural child within each of us"

1202
"the natural, eternal child within us"

1203
"the natural heritage of each living person"

1204
"the natural instinct that propels us toward creation, choice, liberation and change"

1205
"the natural potential that is part of the self"

1206
"the natural principle [sic] underlying all existence from the smallest cell to the largest social organism"

1207
"the natural right [sic] of man"

1208
"the nature of human nature"

1209
"the nature of man"

1210
"the … nature of man, which we must consider fixed and unalterable … the natural urges which are characteristic of the human species"

Creating the Future is everyone's business because everyone is going to live there.

August T. Jaccaci

1211
"the natural patterns in our lives"

1212
"the need [sic] all children have in common … the need to develop to the full extent of their talents"

1213
"the need for self-worth and self-esteem in all of us … the desire of individuals to achieve and maintain a sense of personal worth and importance [that] motivates them to want to be valued"

1214
"the needs of the human being … his basic urges … his tendencies toward … uniqueness; ... to be worth something to other people … to hold in his hands the results of his handiwork, and call them good; to be captain of his own soul; to feel deeply the wholeness of his relationships with life"

1215
"the noblest human qualities alone capable of assuring him a happiness worthy of him"

1216
"the noblest trait in human nature, the trait which above all others links man most clearly to the divine task of evolution"

1217
"the object of your life"

1218
"the obvious, persistent indications of soul"

1219
"the one Great Work of the universe"

1220
"the one imperative of Existence"

We cannot fool ourselves for long about what we are to do. Somewhere deep down in us is stored the secret, and when we are digging in the wrong place, we know it. The secret wants to be discovered and will not let us go in peace a way that is not ours.

Elizabeth O'Connor

1221
"the one project that means more to you than anything in the world"

1222
"the one sovereign motivation that gives direction and unity to one's life"

1223
"the one thing I must do before I die"

1224
"the one thing that gives each of us his worth"

1225
"the one thing that gives me the most joy"

1226
"the one thing that is worth waking up for … task you look forward to"

1227
"the only [activity] which gives man a reason for existence and attributes a definite significance to his life"

1228
"the only drive by which the life of an organism is determined"

1229
"the only end of life: [sic] to be what we are and to become what we are capable of becoming"

1230
"the only natural and authentic way for human beings to live"

No fundamental redressment of the world conditions and human prospects is possible except by worldwide cooperation in a global context and with long views.

The Club of Rome

1231
"the only work of the universe"

1232
"the opportunity to birth what we can of greatness, to join our … work to the Great Work of the universe"

1233
"the optimal state of being"

1234
"the originative power of life, which we may and commonly do neglect"

1235
"the part [we, each] can and must play in life, if our present … civilization is to endure"

1236
"the part of [a person] that is essential to his being human"

1237
"the part of [us] that strives for the highest"

1238
"the particular paradeigma that is your lot"

1239
"the particularity you feel to be you"

1240
"the passion that burns inside you and the issues of the world that animate you"

When society requires to be rebuilt, there is no use in attempting to rebuild it on the old plan.

John Stuart Mill

1241
"the passion that urges us to create, to display, to tell our story … to become part of the revelatory history of the universe"

1242
"the passion to make a difference"

1243
"the path I ought to follow"

1244
"the path of the soul's purpose"

1245
"the personal and the eternal truth of who we are"

1246
"the personal equation"

1247
"the personal [sense of] responsibility that defies all the homicidal prompting of reasonable [rational] calculation"

1248
"the pioneering spirit required by humanity in the twenty-first century"

1249
"the place of humanity in the scheme of things"

1250
"the possibilities that are in each person"

In order to make a viable creative contribution one must change both the symbolic system and the social system at the same time. It is not enough to come up with new ideas, new facts, new laws. One also must convince … people that they will be able to make a living and a name for themselves by adopting the new perspective.

E. O. Wilson

1251
"the possibilities your life holds"

1252
"the potential for good in every person"

1253
"the potential to change the world [that] each of us has [sic]"

1254
"the potentiality afforded by individual diversity"

1255
"the power behind everything [we do]"

1256
"the power behind our purpose"

1257
"the power to continuously reinvent and renew ourselves"

1258
"the power to make a difference – in our lives and our world"

1259
"the powerful latency which is within you"

1260
"the powerful tendency, inherent in all living things, to progress, to evolve, to move toward a state of fulfillment"

All human beings have some spark of creativeness within them. … Both home and the school have the responsibility of encouraging this innate creativeness of the child and of giving it opportunity to develop.

Stanwood Cobb

1261
"the presence within us all of a 'man within the breast' … It is the love of what is honorable and noble, of the grandeur and dignity, and superiority of our own characters"

1262
"the pressure toward fuller and fuller being, more and more perfect actualization of one's humanness"

1263
"the primary motivation of human action"

1264
"the primary motivational force in man [sic] striving to find a meaning in one's life"

1265
"the primary purpose of life"

1266
"the principal quality of being human"

1267
"the principle [sic] guiding human life within the very structure and functioning of the universe itself"

1268
"the promptings of the soul"

1269
"the psychic dimension of our lives"

1270
"the psychological substratum of the human personality whose presence we have come to recognize in many areas of behavior"

Were it not for slow, painful, and constantly discouraged creative effort, man would be no more than a species of primate living on seeds, fruit, roots, and uncooked flesh.

James Harvey Robinson

1271
"the purpose of each soul"

1272
"the purpose of life we all share ... making the infinite finite – bringing spiritual qualities into individual expression"

1273
"the purpose of my life"

1274
"the purpose of your existence [which] is ... to actualize your ... human potentials"

1275
"the purposive, goal-directed activity inherent in living things, from the unfolding of a seed to man's pursuit of his highest aspirations"

1276
"the push toward growth [that] lies within each child ... an inner timetable for growth – a pattern unique to him"

1277
"the qualities that make [us] unique human beings and [our] lives worth living"

1278
"the quest for work that has meaning ... a powerful driving force that, for many, goes unsatisfied"

1279
"the quest ... the search for our true selves"

1280
"the quest for meaning"

The world would be a very different place if it were not for creativity. We would still act according to the few clear instructions our genes contain ... There is no question that the human species could not survive, either now or in the years to come, if creativity were to dry out.

Mihaly Csikszentmihalyi

1281
"the quest for purpose"

1282
"the quest of man"

1283
"the quest to validate the self [that] might lead to great achievements"

1284
"the real inner effort toward improvement"

1285
"the real nature of man"

1286
"the real needs of human nature"

1287
"the real me"

1288
"the real self"

1289
"the 'real you' … a unique and intuitive being with a tremendous capacity to create positive change in the world"

1290
"the realization of our soul's purpose"

Our first task … is to nurture our own and other's creativity, and to whatever extent we succeed in becoming creative persons, everything that we do will have marks of creativity. To be creative is our first aim; to do creatively is the second.

Reuel L. Howe

1291
"the realization of the individual"

1292
"[the] reason for [our] being alive at all"

1293
"the Reason that manifests itself [throughout] nature"

1294
"the resplendent dimensions of the self"

1295
"the richly varied potentialities of mankind"

1296
"the root of the tree of life, the ultimate cause of all the innumerable effects which constitute the relative field of life"

1297
"the sacred in human life"

1298
"the sacredness of each individual life"

1299
"the satisfaction of knowing that [one's] life would mean something"

1300
"the search for the discovery of meaning in life"

To the extent that the intrinsic nature of the individual is nourished and cultivated, the person maintains his integrity, and moves toward originality of expression and actualization of his potentialities.

Clark E. Moustakas

1301
"the seed of inner greatness, our true essence"

1302
"the seeds now dormant in man's nature"

1303
"the self – something inside us directing [our] consciousness"

1304
"the self's fundamental sense of connection"

1305
"the sense of fulfillment … when we are engaged in an activity that we feel important, meaningful to us, … worth doing, [and] intrinsically rewarding, in and of itself"

1306
"the sense of fulfillment, with its consequent peace of mind [that] comes to us only when our ways of living and our accomplishments are in harmony with our deeper inner purposes"

1307
"the sense of individuality at the core of 'me'"

1308
"the sense of meaning that people derive from their jobs"

1309
"the sense of mission, of being in tune with the forces of nature"

1310
"[the] sense of selfness WITH others"

We yearn excessively for entertainment, power, intimacy, sexual fulfillment, and material things, and we think we can find these things if we discover the right relationship or job, the right church or therapy. But without soul, whatever we find will be unsatisfying, for what we truly long for is the soul in each of these areas. Lacking that soulfulness, we attempt to gather these alluring satisfactions to us in great masses, thinking apparently that quantity will make up for lack of quality.

Thomas Moore

1311
"thc [sic] scnsc that [wc] arc indccd part of a vast and amazing story – the universe story"

1312
"the significance of every human life"

1313
"the silent, unconscious, unseen influence of [our] life"

1314
"the single most powerful force shaping our lives"

1315
"the single principle underlying all creation, the laws of nature"

1316
"the soul that lies hidden in the everyday and commonplace"

1317
"the soul's code"

1318
"the soul's opus"

1319
"the soul"

1320
"[the] soul-companion, the daimon"

Success has an added ingredient that is indispensable to it. It contains a subjective factor which might be described as the individual's coming to terms with himself and his life through what he is and does. It is a matter of establishing a relationship with life that is both materially and spiritually satisfying. Accomplishment is among the media we use to establish this relationship. But unless our accomplishments give meaning and significance to our lives; unless they give us a sense of self-fulfillment; unless in their totality they give us peace of mind, they cannot be considered as being synonymous with real success. Peace of mind comes to us only when our ways of living and our accomplishments are in harmony with our deeper inner purposes. … The nature of the human being is manifestly such that man cannot get the sense of self-fulfillment, with its consequent peace of mind, out of ends that are solely self-centered.

Lawrence Welk

1321
"the source of divine hope and energy in ourselves"

1322
"the sovereign purpose of life, to actualize oneself"

1323
"the spark of divinity … in everybody"

1324
"the sparks within us"

1325
"the special character of the individual [sic]"

1326
"the special meaning of your own life"

1327
"the special mix that makes up our soul"

1328
"the spirit center of life [that] urges the person to seek meaning, transforming the psychological potential into an actual person in search of the meaning of existence"

1329
"the spirit center of life [that] urges the person to seek meaning, transforming the psychological potential into an actual person in search of the meaning of existence"

1330
"the spirit of Mankind suddenly alive with the sense of all that remains to be done if it is to achieve the fullness of its powers and possibilities"

When soul is neglected, it doesn't just go away; it appears symptomatically in obsessions, addictions, violence, and loss of meaning. Our temptation is to isolate these symptoms or to try to eliminate them one by one; but the root problem is that we have lost our wisdom about the soul, even our interest in it.

Thomas Moore

1331
"the spirited form that lies within"

1332
"the spiritual core ... the very best of who we are"

1333
"the spiritual fire without which all material fires, so laboriously lighted, will presently die down on the surface of the thinking earth"

1334
"the spiritual nature of man"

1335
"the spiritual power of human beings"

1336
"the spiritual purposes for which [each of us] was born"

1337
"the spiritual reality that is the source of all consciousness"

1338
"the spiritual union of our passion with our essential, inherent talents which results in a perfect alignment of spirit with function"

1339
"the spiritual values of life ... that will benefit both ourselves and our fellow creatures"

1340
"the springs of human actions"

It is difficult, if not impossible, for most people to think otherwise than in the fashion of their own period.

George Bernard Shaw

1341
"the still small voice within [that] always tells us the truth"

1342
"the still small voice within that speaks to you in images, wishes, dreams and fantasies"

1343
"the ... still untapped forces that lie with the human being himself; energies capable of leading humanity away from destruction toward eventual 'liberation and realization'"

1344
"the storehouse of internal wisdom"

1345
"the story that only you could write ... the story that resides in [your] well and [that] other people will never be able to draw up"

1346
"the striving to find a meaning in one's life"

1347
"the strongest force in human life"

1348
"the strongest of all our value drives, the one which ultimately shapes all the rest"

1349
"the subjective wisdom within you"

1350
"the successful use of our strengths"

Each of us can make a difference.

Gerald G. Jampolsky

1351
"the superordinate directionality (or directionalities) of [a person's] activities, whether mental, verbal, or physical"

1352
"the supreme light in all [of us]"

1353
"the supreme object of [life] for all people"

1354
"the talented, creative nature that lives in each of us – something that is ready to accomplish a great purpose"

1355
"[the] tendency of the mind to flow toward more and more growth, toward fulfillment"

1356
"the tendency to actualize, as much as possible, [the organism's] individual capacities"

1357
"the thing in this world which is of most supreme importance, indeed the thing which is of most practical value to the race"

1358
"the timeless aspect of life that brings what everyone dreams of – pure love, pure joy, pure fulfillment in spirit"

1359
"[the] timeless dimension of being"

1360
"the timeless source of our being"

Learn to repeat endlessly to yourself, "it all depends on me."

André Gide

1361
"the timeless, the unchanging, the unborn, at our very center"

1362
"the tools you are given to affect the world"

1363
"the transcendent level of consciousness … a mode of consciousness in which the individual feels connected to the cosmos as a whole"

1364
"the transcendent self … [using one's] finely honed uniqueness for the common good"

1365
"the transpersonal dimensions of existence"

1366
"the tremendous dynamo of energy and intelligence within man [that] is constantly empowering and directing human activity"

1367
"the true … life-roles"

1368
"the true greatness within us"

1369
"the true nature of man"

1370
"the true plan of [your] life"

*We are suffering from a metaphysical disease,
and the cure must therefore be metaphysical.*

E. F. Schumacher

1371
"the true pulse of life itself"

1372
"the true value of men"

1373
"the truly human way"

1374
"the truth of one's being"

1375
"the ultimate and fundamental ends"

1376
"the ultimate answer to basic fulfillment"

1377
"the ultimate answer to being human"

1378
"the ultimate end of human experience"

1379
"the ultimate end of human life"

1380
"the ultimate freedom; the last inner freedom … that makes life meaningful and purposeful [and that] cannot be lost [or] taken away"

If we are to break habit-sets and move into new, original ways of viewing our problems and challenges, we must find ways to break old mental associations or connections and form new ones.

Sidney J. Parnes

1381
"[the] ultimate meaning"

1382
"the ultimate motivation ... the need for self-esteem, the powerful, innate desire to be satisfied with one's self"

1383
"the ultimate mysteries that frame a human life"

1384
"the ultimate nature of life ... what life is, what man is, what the universe is"

1385
"the ultimate point of fulfillment or actualization of [one's] genetic potential"

1386
"the ultimate question [sic] of life"

1387
"the ultimate source of [our] power"

1388
"the ultimate work ... an engagement with soul"

1389
"the unalterable demands of life itself"

1390
"the unbounded nature of your being"

Man always looks at nature through coloured glasses ... even when he is not conscious of it and believes that he is engaged in 'pure vision', unsullied by any meaning. The 'innocent eye' is a fiction, based on the absurd notion that what we perceive in the present can be isolated in the mind from the influence of past experience. There is no perception of 'pure form' but meaning seeps in, and settles on the image ...

Arthur Koestler

1391
"the unchanging truth"

1392
"the unconditioned spirit trapped in conditions, like the sun in eclipse"

1393
"the unconscious predispositions that shape our everyday experiences"

1394
"the underlying and unlimited intelligence that resides within all of us – in our hearts and souls"

1395
"the underlying essence of who we are"

1396
"the underlying purpose and values that motivate an individual"

1397
"the undying spirit that informs the surface forms of our life"

1398
"the unfathomable mystery that is the very seed and heart of each individual"

1399
"the unfolding of … individual patterns, the kind of person [one] is, and the direction in which he can move"

1400
"the unfolding of the … artistic [sic] and spiritual potentials that lie within all of us"

If language be not in accordance with the truth of thing, affairs cannot be carried on to success.

Confucius

1401
"the unfolding of the maximum individual potential"

1402
"the unfolding of the meaning of our lives … what we do … to actualize our potential"

1403
"the unique inner consciousness which serves to navigate the living vessel of each life back to the safe harbor of reunion with the divine love which sent it forth"

1404
"the unique mark each of us makes in the world"

1405
"the unique and the universal in the individual and in mankind"

1406
"the unique snowflake nature of individuals"

1407
"the unique stamp that is your personality"

1408
"the unique way that your own life can unfold"

1409
"the uniquely human potential at its best … to transform a personal tragedy into triumph, to turn one's predicament into a human achievement"

1410
"the uniqueness of a person"

Every engineer, every scientist, every farmer, every mechanic knows that nothing will work, that no act will succeed, unless it is in harmony with rightness – the true nature of things as they are.

Henry Grady Weaver

1411
"the uniqueness within [each of us]"

1412
"the uniqueness within you that calls to be lived"

1413
"the universal growth forces within [the individual]"

1414
"the universal need for psychological nurturance and individual growth"

1415
"the universal Self in us"

1416
"the unquenchable curiosity which the student has as a small child"

1417
"the unused energies of the human mind [that will always] find an outlet in spite of every comfort and every distraction"

1418
"the urge for self-transcendence"

1419
"the urge to grow, the pressure to self-actualization, the quest for one's identity"

1420
"the value of each individual citizen"

Do not hire a man who does your work for money, but him who does it for love of it.

Henry David Thoreau

1421
"the variety in aptitude and capabilities and desires that each and every one of us has [sic]"

1422
"the vast potential that our humanity gives us as a birthright"

1423
"the vast treasure of what it is to be human"

1424
"the vast untapped energy within you"

1425
"the very foundation of [our] being"

1426
"the very meaning and value of our lives"

1427
"the very nature of our human mode of being"

1428
"the very purpose of our existence"

1429
"the very root of [our] being"

1430
"the very soul of humankind [that] is crying out to be expressed, … to be made fully alive through giving to others"

Those with views and values at variance with the prevailing world-order consensus need to be particularly imaginative and dedicated to obtain a fair hearing. Governmental efforts all over the world to induce media to conform to official ideology suggest the difficulty facing those who seek to promote changes in the … system.

Richard A. Falk

1431
“the very special gifts you have to offer [to the world]”

1432
“the very substance of life”

1433
“the very thing that defines who and what you are”

1434
“the voice in your head that answers a question you ask yourself [sic]”

1435
“the voice of God in our lives”

1436
“the voice of the nonphysical world”

1437
“the voice of your soul”

1438
“the voice within you”

1439
“the wealth of abilities and traits within the individual that [only need community stimulation and support] to achieve their full degree of differentiation”

1440
“the wellspring of all our actions”

If we accept that all original thinking and all new ideas came from the mind of some individual at sometime and someplace, then the importance of a creative climate in organizations and institutions everywhere that permits individuals to participate with their thinking is better appreciated.

Richard J. Spady and Cecil H. Bell

1441
"the well-springs of [our] being"

1442
"the wellsprings of a full human life"

1443
"the 'why' or underlying impellents of behavior"

1444
"the will to make a difference"

1445
"the will-to-meaning"

1446
"the wisdom and intelligence of our hearts"

1447
"the wisdom inherent in our bodies"

1448
"the wisdom of our true natures"

1449
"the wish to grow … to become 'what we are'"

1450
"the wizard within all of us [that] sees and knows everything"

No man ever disappears completely if he strives to do good and expects no reward outside of the joy of having contributed to the progress of mankind. Our intellectual endeavors, our whole science will be of no avail if they do not lead man to a better comprehension of himself, of the meaning of his life, and of the resources buried in his inner self.

Lecomte du Noüy

1451
"the wonder and beauty we bring to the world through how we give our attention to a piece of music, a flower, or a tree"

1452
"the work of the universe"

1453
"the work that is ours to do"

1454
"the work we [each] have been called to do"

1455
"the work we [sic] love and have [sic] taken positive steps to realize it"

1456
"the work we were made for"

1457
"the work you have accomplished that would not have been done by someone else"

1458
"the yearning to leave [one's] piece of the world a better place for [one's] children and grandchildren"

1459
"the yearnings of [our] soul[s]"

1460
"the you of you"

It isn't that [we] can't see the solution. It is that [we] can't see the problem.

G. K. Chesterton

1461

"these fundamental dimensions of experience [which are] natural to a child"

1462

"things for which we appear to have the most ability and interest"

1463

"things that are both … gratifying and at the same time … necessary for creating a more harmonious future"

1464

"things we have to do [sic] in order to fulfill our missions"

1465

"things you naturally do well"

1466

"this distinctively human capacity"

1467

"this energy that guides our work"

1468

"this field of unlimited potential [utilization of which] all aspects of [a person's] life flourish, in the same way that the branches, fruits and leaves of a tree flourish when the roots maintain contact with the field of nourishment in the soil"

1469

"this impetus which must be maintained in the heart of Man and encouraged to grow at all costs … if Evolution is to continue"

1470

"this impulse … for self-fulfillment [sic]"

We need constantly to be on the lookout for new ways of defining problems in order to keep up with the demands life keeps placing on us.

Robert J. Sternberg and Todd I. Lubart

1471

“this [self-actualizing] urge that every human being has [sic] as his or her birthright [which] can be squelched and corrupted, but … cannot be completely extinguished”

1472

“this spark in ourselves [that] makes [sic] us the one we were meant to be”

1473

“this striving to find meaning in one’s life [which] is the primary motivational force in man”

1474

“this urgent march of the [human] mind – imperfect but marvelous, unique in every individual – which has brought us out of savagery toward civilization and wisdom, and will take us further still”

1475

“this uniqueness and singleness which distinguishes each individual and gives a meaning to his existence”

1476

“those areas which are of the most interest and are the most fulfilling”

1477

“those goals which the center [sic] gives to your life”

1478

“those parts of the self that transcend the limits of ego”

1479

“those powers which constitute the vital principle of the soul”

1480

“to be constructively influential in the world … a factor in bettering world conditions … bringing [sic] harmony … helping others to be free and spontaneous … being in tune with nature … helping others live better … exercising an important influence in [our] society and on the whole world”

Problems may be solved only when the appropriate techniques, data, theories, or concepts are invented to solve them.

Robert Scott Root-Bernstein

1481
"to be engaged, to be involved fully and consciously rather than passively in the [sic] integrative process between man and his environment"

1482
"to be truly human and, therefore, fully alive and conscious of [our] consciousness and potentials"

1483
"to live in accordance with one's true nature"

1484
"to really participate in the divine task"

1485
"to think what nobody has yet thought about that which everybody sees"

1486
"transcendent function"

1487
"transcendent maturation and successful conscious evolution"

1488
"transcendent qualities of life"

1489
"true being [that] precedes true action"

1490
"true work [that] comes from our being"

If we can really understand the problem, the answer will come out of it, because the answer is not separate from the problem.

Jiddu Krishnamurti

1491
"true work of the universe"

1492
"Truthful Effort [with] inbred pleasure to it, a spontaneity, a sense of being one with the activity"

1493
"ultimate meanings or eternal values"

1494
"unconscious determinants of behavior"

1495
"understand[ing] and fulfill[ing] our assigned role"

1496
"understanding your own unique strengths and emphasizing them, not trying to remake yourself into somebody else"

1497
"unfinished life processes that are [sic] inherent in the human organism"

1498
"unfolding [or] acting out our being"

1499
"unfold[ing] more of man's latent potential"

1500
"unified flow experience … that harmony [where a person's] … feelings, thoughts, and actions are congruent with one another"

Before Newton identified gravity, apples fell off trees all the time but people had no name or explanation for what was happening.

Riane Eisler

1501

"union with the deeper structures of reality ... union with the human community ... union with the Earth, with the universe itself in the full wonder of its being"

1502

"unique skills and talents that we each have [sic] that can serve the world around us, and bring betterment to the planet"

1503

"unlimited desire and interest of children to know and to do and to be"

1504

"universal responsibility ... everyone shares for the present and future well-being of the human family and the larger living world"

1505

"unmet human needs for emotional and spiritual fulfillment [sic]"

1506

"unmet human needs ... the emotional and spiritual fulfillment missing from a system rooted in fear and force"

1507

"unity with life"

1508

"untold potentials of the mind [that] can create new niches, occupations, roles ... and numerous semi-natural and synthetic physical environments as well"

1509

"unused resources within us [which] if tapped, could [sic] put an end to suffering"

1510

"using my gifts to add real value to people's lives"

The tragedy of life doesn't lie in not reaching your goal. The tragedy lies in having no goal to reach.

Benjamin E. Mays

1511
"using our gifts toward some end that moves us"

1512
"using the resources of your soul to fulfill what you were born to do"

1513
"using your talents and abilities – your gifts – to better not only your life, but the lives of those around you"

1514
"vision … that is true to life, to the imperatives of creation and evolution"

1515
"ways of being that help us free ourselves of the dead hand of the past"

1516
"wellspring of human growth and change"

1517
"what [a person] is potentially"

1518
"what being human means"

1519
"what comes naturally"

1520
"what comes to [us] from the depths"

It is imperative to reappraise the scale of the usual human values. … Even if we are spared destruction by war, life will have to change in order not to perish on its own. We cannot avoid reassessing the fundamental definitions of human life and human society.

Aleksandr I. Solzhenitsyn

1521
"what, deep down, we really want"

1522
"what distinguishes us from other life forms"

1523
"what distinguishes you from others"

1524
"what each of us loves"

1525
"what [each soul] seeks to accomplish"

1526
"what feels not just familiar, but deeply true and right when we do it"

1527
"what gives meaning to your own life"

1528
"what has been lost of our intrinsic selves"

1529
"what human life is really about"

1530
"what human nature really is when it is given full expression"

The growth of civilization is the work of creative personalities and creative minorities; these cannot go on moving forward themselves unless they contrive to carry their fellows with them in their advance.

Arnold Toynbee

1531
"what I am [sic] meant to do here"

1532
"what I am [sic] supposed to do with my life"

1533
"what I most yearn to give my full energy and commitment"

1534
"what I really want in my life"

1535
"what I want to do for the rest of my life"

1536
"what I would be doing, if I knew I could not fail"

1537
"what, in the spiritual sense, we are all here for"

1538
"what is authentic and genuine in man"

1539
"what is best in man"

1540
"what is calling us to act [sic] and how we can answer"

We want the generous impulse to act that which we imagine; we want the poetry of life: our calculations have outrun conception; we have eaten more than we can digest. The cultivation of those sciences which have enlarged the Empire of man over the external world, has, for want of the poetical faculty, proportionately circumscribed those of the internal world; and man, having enslaved the elements, remains himself a slave.

Percy Bysshe Shelly

1541
"what is essential about the human person"

1542
"what is genuine, what is genuinely human, in man"

1543
"what is more than genetically encoded in us"

1544
"what is most important for our lives"

1545
"what is most important in life, [sic] what directs our actions – [sic] how we think, why we feel the way we feel"

1546
"what is peculiar and idiosyncratic in people [sic] … the quirks in their personality which make [sic] them different and original"

1547
"what is real and most meaningful"

1548
"what is real in me"

1549
"what is special about humankind"

1550
"what is special to each of [us]"

Passion is not invulnerable. Even the most strongly motivated children can be seriously undermined by inhibiting environments and, as a result, their creativity can be killed.

Teresa Amabile

1551
"what [is] timeless and immutable about human ... existence"

1552
"what is true and unifying"

1553
"what is truly innate"

1554
"what is unique and particular to the individual"

1555
"what is vital to you"

1556
"what is worth striving for"

1557
"what it is that gives meaning and joy to your life"

1558
"what it is that keeps alive in some people the natural spark of curiosity, eagerness, hunger for life and experience"

1559
"what it is that we love to do so that our life on the purely physical plane will have resonances within our innermost being and reality, so that we feel the rapture of being alive"

1560
"what it is that you would do with your life even if you didn't get paid for it"

Any group, organization, community, or society which inhibits the free movement of ideas of its members up, down, and across its organizational and social structures (whether innocently or not) is depriving itself of its greatest resource – human thought – and is in grave danger of being buried in history by an avalanche of the creativity of others.

Richard J. Spady

1561
"what it is to be fully and functionally human"

1562
"what it is to be human"

1563
"what it is [sic] you are called to follow, even when it feels like you are following the free and erratic flight of a wild bird"

1564
"what it is you are here in the earth to do"

1565
"what it is you enjoy so much that you lose tract of time when you're doing it"

1566
"what it means to be human"

1567
"what it means to burst at the seams"

1568
"what it means to 'work without a why' .. [to] work for the sake of working"

1569
"what life is for … why it is given"

1570
"what makes a society 'good,' or in line with the course of evolution"

Carrying out the Great Work of making an ecologically durable and decent society will require us to confront the deeper cultural roots of our problems and grow out of the faith that we can meet the challenge of sustainability without really changing much. The evidence … shows that we will have to change a great deal and mostly in ways that we will come to regard as vastly better than what exists now and certainly better than what is in prospect. This is a design challenge like no other.

David Orr

1571
"what makes me, me"

1572
"what makes my life matter; what makes it more than mere biological existence"

1573
"what makes one day different from the next"

1574
"what makes the human being unique and wondrous"

1575
"what makes us act as we do"

1576
"what makes us more deeply human"

1577
"what makes you uniquely human [which] you need to employ … in all your human affairs"

1578
"what makes you, you and makes you unique"

1579
"what man is [sic] at his best"

1580
"what most distinguishes us as humans"

By seeing the larger patterns, we can take effective action, moving beyond competition to cooperation, harmonizing with the natural principles underlying all existence from the smallest cell to the largest social organism.

Diane Dreher

1581
"what motivates you, what brings fulfillment"

1582
"what one is called to do, which may or may not coincide with one's occupation, with what one is actually doing"

1583
"what one is really like inside, deep down, as a member of the human species"

1584
"what – or who – each of us individually is"

1585
"what our hearts are directing us to do"

1586
"what [people] deeply care about, what gives their life passionate meaning"

1587
"what [people] like to do and what they have a gift for doing"

1588
"what people truly and most deeply want"

1589
"what people would like to become if they could"

1590
"what provides fulfillment"

Neither position nor power, wealth nor geography will protect us from the inadequacies of our traditional ways of solving problems … or the false assumptions that undergird those methods. The flaws are not just inadequate, they can be fatal.

George Land and Beth Jarman

1591
"what pushes you when you are alone with yourself"

1592
"what really makes your heart sing"

1593
"what resonates in your being and calls forth a response on your part"

1594
"what seems different in yourself … the rare thing you possess"

1595
"what the daimon demands"

1596
"what the spirit demands from [each of us], what the age would like to make impossible"

1597
"what the spiritual life is all about"

1598
"what truly matters to you"

1599
"what ultimately human life is all about"

1600
"what we are best cut out for … domains we have affinity for"

We tend to think of innovators as those who contribute to a new way of doing things. But many far-reaching changes have been touched off by those who contribute to a new way of thinking about things.

John W. Gardner

1601
"what we are here for"

1602
"what [we] are here to give"

1603
"what we are living for"

1604
"what we are potentially"

1605
"what we are that brings meaning and purpose"

1606
"what we are to be … how we are to be it"

1607
"what we are to do in life"

1608
"what we are to do with our life"

1609
"what we are willing to commit ourselves to … what will stir up our deepest motives"

1610
"what we can [sic] do that will fill our lives with meaning"

In most people creativity is imprisoned behind walls built of self-imposed constraints. Such constraints convert simple problems into unsolvable puzzles.

Russell L. Ackoff

1611
"what we do well and enjoy doing"

1612
"what we have to give this world and one another"

1613
"what we know in our hearts we ought to be doing"

1614
"what we leave behind"

1615
"what we used to be when we were human"

1616
"what we value, what we hold sacred, what puts spirit into our lives"

1617
"what [we] wanted most in life … things [we] most wanted to do in the limited time that [we] had"

1618
"what, without you, might never have been seen"

1619
"what you actually are"

1620
"what you are [sic] here to be and do in this life"

I believe that the Universe is basically good and that throughout its great forces are at work striving to bring about a greater unity of all living things. It is through cooperation with these forces that Man will achieve all of which he is capable.

Kenneth Kaunda

1621

“what you are naturally good at”

1622

“what you can be”

1623

“what you can contribute to make a difference”

1624

“what you can do [sic] to support positive change close to home”

1625

“what you care about, what you love, what you are passionate about”

1626

“what you consider to be eternally significant”

1627

“what you do best and enjoy most”

1628

“what … you DO, here on this earth, here in your life … your work … your passion … your aspiration … your dream …your calling”

1629

“what you do well and love”

1630

“what you enjoy doing, what you’re adept at”

It is now time to ask the universe a new cosmological question: "What is Love?" No longer is it the job of one man alone to ask, but the job of all humanity.

August T. Jaccaci

1631
"what you love to do … what you naturally do well and what you have been doing all your life, although for most of your life you have probably done it without thinking of being compensated"

1632
"what … you most enjoy after work … what you most want to do on weekends and vacations … your hobbies … your extracurricular activities .. what you love to do for yourself"

1633
"what you shine at doing … what makes your brain light up"

1634
"what you want to dedicate your energy to [sic] what you want to create during your lifetime [sic] what you want to create that will last beyond your lifetime [sic]"

1635
"what you want to give to the world"

1636
"what you were born to do"

1637
"what [your] heart is telling [you] to do"

1638
"what your … life is about"

1639
"what your unique talents are"

1640
"what's unique about you"

Every individual is of value. … If we believe what we profess concerning the worth of the individual, then the idea of individual fulfillment within a framework of moral purpose must become our deepest concern, our [global] preoccupation, our passion, our obsession.

John W. Gardner

1641

"whatever directs the development of an [individual] towards goals set up within [his or her] living stuff. It is present in all of life ... [and] rooted in purpose"

1642

"when I can be real, when I can be close to whatever it is that is going on within me"

1643

"when our inner self connects to our work and our work to our inner self [and] the work knows no limit, for the inner self knows no limit"

1644

"when our work joins the great work of creation and we become great ourselves"

1645

"when the search for our own truth is our work"

1646

"where we are ourselves"

1647

"where your 'center' is"

1648

"who and what you really are"

1649

"who I am ... the cry of Everyman ... the ultimate question for which theologian, philosopher, artist, psychologist, and social scientist have sought adequate answers"

1650

"who we are and why we live"

If society wants an abundant harvest of creativeness, it must prepare fertile fields, spread … the seeds of general culture, and offer a receptive and appreciative market for the growth of talent and of genius. And fortunately, what society most wants in any epoch, it somehow has the power to evoke! … But if human society depends upon genius for its progress, genius itself is dependent upon society for its stimuli and opportunities. Strive as it will, genius cannot successfully function in an environment totally unfavorable to it.

Stanwood Cobb

1651
"who we are as spiritually developing human beings"

1652
"who we are at the core"

1653
"who we really are"

1654
"who we truly are – souls seeking to grow"

1655
"who, what, and why you are"

1656
"who you are and what you have to offer the world"

1657
"who you are and what you have to share"

1658
"who you are at a deep level and what your life, at best, should really be about"

1659
"who you are deep down, and who others are"

1660
"why I am on the planet at this time"

Even the greatest genius will not accomplish anything without the support of society and culture.

Mihaly Csikszentmihalyi

1661
"why I was put here"

1662
"why we exist"

1663
"why we were born"

1664
"why you are who you are … your own traits and preferences"

1665
"willing[ness] to reclaim our story for ourselves"

1666
"win[ning] a victory over yourself, widen[ing] your vision and your world, walk[ing] into a new and fuller life"

1667
"work for which [one] has affinity"

1668
"work that [is] … personally authentic and expressive of [our] … selves"

1669
"work that is unique to you … that you are called to do"

1670
"work [that is] valued … meaningful …useful … satisfying … and [that] use[s] your potential"

We must indeed take a strong stand against the implications, however they may creep in, that talent is a disease and creativity is a neurosis.

Rollo May

1671
"work [that provides the worker] with an authentic vida positiva … joy … awe … bliss … ecstasy … a sense of transcendence, a sense of deep meaning and connectedness"

1672
"work that satisfies the soul"

1673
"working for change in the world"

1674
"working … from our inner selves"

1675
"work[ing] to make all other individuals successful"

1676
"worthwhile challenges that we feel natural passion for"

1677
"your authentic self"

1678
"your being, that which is authentically you"

1679
"your best destiny"

1680
"your calling in life"

The human personality craves the sense of growth, of realization of personal powers, and it suffers in an environment that denies growth or frustrates it erratically or for reasons other than the similar needs for growth in others.

Robert S. Lynd

1681
"your center, your identity, your totality of self"

1682
"your central purpose as a soul in this lifetime"

1683
"[your] childhood impulses ... what you really wanted to do as a child"

1684
"your configuration ... the lot your soul chose before you ever took a breath"

1685
"your contribution to the world around you"

1686
"your core passion"

1687
"your deepest energies"

1688
"your deepest sense of truth"

1689
"your Destiny, Cause, and Calling"

1690
"your divine purpose"

If we make radical changes in our beliefs about human capacity, we can break through to a new way of life.

Doris J. Shallcross and Dorothy A. Sisk

1691
"your drives, your beliefs, your desires … where your stories happen"

1692
"your gift to the world"

1693
"your gifts … how you can [sic] best serve"

1694
"your heart's calling … your own inner voice"

1695
"your higher nature … who and what you really are"

1696
"your highest ideals and wishes [which] stand above the commonplace"

1697
"your highest purpose in life"

1698
"your highest self"

1699
"your individuality"

1700
"your inherent abilities"

Beware the symptomatic solution. Solutions that address only the symptoms of a problem, not fundamental causes, tend to have short-term benefits at best. In the long term, the problem resurfaces and there is increased pressure for symptomatic response. Meanwhile, the capacity for fundamental solutions can atrophy.

Peter M. Senge

1701
"your inner compass"

1702
"your inner powers"

1703
"your inner resources and … the 'calling' that can lead you to happiness and fulfillment"

1704
"your inner self"

1705
"your innermost resources"

1706
"[your] internal companion"

1707
"your internal compass"

1708
"your intuitive self"

1709
"your journey of authentic experience"

1710
"your life task"

Everyone has, simply by existing, a right to be intelligent. And to be provided with a way to become consistently more intelligent. This is a right that must be recognized and held sacred. Above all, the necessary conditions for the exercise of this right must be available. This is society's mission and the primary obligation of its leaders. All of them.

Luis Machado

1711
"your life's calling"

1712
"your [life's] journey"

1713
"your life's work"

1714
"your limitless inner power"

1715
"your loving inner presence"

1716
"your maximum potential"

1717
"your meant-to-be"

1718
"your mission in life"

1719
"your most … ideal intention of service to life"

1720
"your most deeply felt aspirations"

If a great change is to be made in human affairs, the minds of men will be fitted to it; the general opinions and feelings will draw that way. Every fear, every hope will forward it...

Matthew Arnold

1721
"your most essential character as a soul"

1722
"your most precious resource"

1723
"your music"

1724
"your niche in life"

1725
"your overall goal"

1726
"your own authentic self – your Higher Self"

1727
"your own inner Essence"

1728
"your own inner value"

1729
"[your] own internal teacher"

1730
"your own life purpose"

No great improvements in the lot of mankind are possible, until a great change takes place in the fundamental constitution of their modes of thought.

John Stuart Mill

1731
“your own overarching purpose”

1732
“your own potential and passion”

1733
“your own signature on life”

1734
“your own spiritual core”

1735
“your own true nature and purpose in life”

1736
“[your] own true work”

1737
“your own unique gifts”

1738
“your own unique mission in life”

1739
“your path in life”

1740
“your personal destiny”

In the past fifty years we have seen the passing of many classical expressions of literature, science, philosophy and other different dispensations of life which came out of the various civilizations of the past. Newton fell to Einstein, just as Aristotle fell to Galileo and so the pattern goes. Each day finds new concepts, new evaluations, new truths taking the place of those which formerly meant life and death to so many millions of people. On this basis it is quite safe to predict that, in the near future, our modern psychiatry, psychology and medicine will be just as primitive as that which we now consider primitive … which have existed in the past ages.

Ernest L. Norman

1741
"your personal power"

1742
"your place in the universe"

1743
"your purpose in life"

1744
"your Purposed Self"

1745
"your real nature"

1746
"your reason for being"

1747
"your reason to live"

1748
"your role in life"

1749
"your role in the creation process"

1750
"your sacred quest"

The world is faced with challenges that may well imperil civilization as we know it. The old solutions and procedures for dealing with political and social problems no longer appear to work. Hope seems to lie in beginning to seek new creative solutions, new approaches and breakthroughs for the global dilemmas we now face.

Willis Harman

1751
"your soul or your higher self"

1752
"your soul's hunger for meaning and purpose"

1753
"your soul's purpose"

1754
"[your] source of energy and direction"

1755
"your spiritual mission"

1756
"your spiritual reality"

1757
"your true center, the place from which you act as yourself"

1758
"your true north"

1759
"your true self … your real nature"

1760
"your true vocation"

Unless individuals, groups, and nations can imagine, construct, and creatively [devise] new ways of relating to these complex changes [in the world], the lights will go out. Unless man can make new and original adaptations to his environment as rapidly as his science can change the environment, our [civilization] will perish...[and] international annihilation will be the price we pay for a lack of creativity.

Carl R. Rogers

1761
"your ultimate calling"

1762
"your ultimate desires"

1763
"your ultimate freedom as a human being"

1764
"your ultimate potential"

1765
"your undiscovered energy"

1766
"your unique calling"

1767
"your unique contribution"

1768
"[your] unique knowledge that can benefit others when you want to make a difference to them"

1769
"your unique mission"

1770
"your unique point of view"

If, as is generally conceded, the world is in a rather sorry mess, crying for solutions to problems that are staggering in complexity and magnitude, the encouragement of creative thinking would seem to be the most necessary and immediate goal of all concerned people.

George R. Eckstein

1771
“your work … your identity”

If we seriously hope to resolve the chaos the world is facing and to achieve the viable and sustainable global future everybody envisions, what is needed is a social-economic-political system in which all the Earth's seven billion inhabitants are able to develop and to engage their unique abilities in important and beneficial activities and, thus, to experience their lives as having meaning and significance. Necessarily, too, we will need to evolve goals for mankind and Planet Earth that people perceive as giving purpose and direction to their own lives and, therefore, as worthy of the commitment of their time and their creative energies. As far as I can see, there is no viable alternative.

Efiong Etuk

EPILOGUE

No great improvements in the lot of mankind are possible, until a great change takes place in the fundamental constitution of their modes of thought.

--John Stuart Mill

Traditionally, the world has viewed its problems as "economic crisis," "social crisis," "educational crisis," "financial crisis," "political crisis," "environmental crisis," and so on. Based on that perception, several sectoral remedies have been considered and tried. The long history of failed solutions, despite enormous commitment of effort and resources, and the visibly deteriorating human and environmental conditions suggest that we may not be tackling the real crisis but, from all indications, the effects rather than their underlying cause.

Considering the large number of life-threatening "crises" the world is facing *vis à vis* scarce and rapidly dwindling resources, I believe it is time to rethink the human predicament and strategies for its solution. This compendium of insights on human nature is intended to stimulate, as well as to inform, that rethinking. Examination of the insights yields two broad conclusions:

> First, the modern crises and the global predicament are not "economic crisis," "social crisis," "political crisis," or "environmental crisis," *per se.* They are not separate crises, either. And they are not due to the so-called "human propensity to evil." As such, they are not likely going to be resolved within the framework of the prevailing understanding of human nature.
>
> Second, the real but unnoticed and unsuspected crisis that is threatening our collective survival and the future of Planet Earth is a *creativity crisis.* This is the inability of the vast majority of people to develop and to beneficially engage their defining and most important attribute as humans. One result of that deprivation is the spreading epidemic of meaninglessness of which most psychological, social, economic, and political problems are the symptoms or facets.

There are two sides to the global creativity crisis: One side is the seriously flawed but generally accepted conception of human nature as inherently self-centered or self-interested, competitive, adversarial, materialistic, and consumption-driven.

The other side is the institutional structures and operational relationships that have been built on that notion. To the extent that these observations are valid, the best hope of resolving the chaos the world is facing and of building the viable, humanly fulfilling, and sustainable global civilization that everyone hopes to see is, first, to correct the misleading views we hold about ourselves and, second, to conform policies, decisions, and actions to the authentic human essence.

Revealing the Truth about Human Nature provides the logical and necessary starting-point for the vitally important and urgently needed correction. Sequel publications entitled *Mass Creativity: A Global Imperative* (in writing) present the concepts and application tools for translating the new understanding of human nature into the fabric of society – into everyday parental, educational, managerial, political, and care-giving actions.

Revealing the Truth about Human Nature and its sequel are born of the conviction that the more we come to grips with our true nature as humans and our place in the harmony of nature, the more socially and ecologically responsible we are likely to become. *Ipso facto,* the more socially and ecologically responsible we are, the less acquisitive, the less consumption-driven, and the less adversarial we are likely to be. Of course, the less adversarial and the less consumption-driven we are, the better for a finite Planet Earth and for posterity.

My aim in compiling these insights on human nature is, primarily, to inspire a new and authentic way of thinking about ourselves and, ultimately, a new way of being and living that will benefit this generation, benefit future generations of mankind, and benefit the rest of nature. The hope is that the compendium and its sequel:

> Speak personally and deeply to everyone, awakening the part of him or her that is unique and special – what distinguishes him or her from others and from other life forms, what makes his or her life really matter, what makes it, as Harold Kushner puts it, "more than mere biological existence."
>
> Encourage readers to view themselves and others as persons of worth, naturally "equipped" and able to make significant positive contributions to society and the Planet.

Underscore society's primary and essential responsibility to create and maintain enabling context and space in which every member is able to develop and to contribute his or her particular set of abilities.

Ultimately, persuade mankind that it is economically more productive, financially more profitable, socially more progressive, politically more farsighted and more prudent, and ecologically more sustainable to provide the conditions in which people are able to actualize their potential, than to try to solve a plethora of problems – psychological, social, economic, and political – most of which are the symptoms of deprived, meaningless, and impoverishing existence.

Here, in summary, is an open invitation to rethink human nature and to commit to its flourishing. Clearly, this is not a task for social scientists and social philosophers alone; but for all of us – the human family.

Revealing the Truth about Human Nature will have achieved its purpose if the insights that are brought together in this volume: a) sufficiently challenged, intrigued, or provoked a critical mass of people to reevaluate the beliefs we currently hold about ourselves as humans; and b) ultimately, persuaded mankind – as a matter of necessity for our collective survival and further progress – to conform public and private policies, decisions, and actions to our authentic, quintessentially creative nature – *Homo Creativus!*

Sources

Noüy, 1947: viii, 147, 152, 154, 163, 237, 244, 248, 255, 273; Holmes, 1950: 57, 58, 63, 66, 71, 72, 74, 75, 95, 113, 121, 122, 123; Murray, 1951: 276; Kipling, 1952: 158; Tillich, 1952: 51, 52, 153, 154; Einstein, 1954: 11, 31, 36, 42, 43, 153, 154, 184, 186; Allport, 1955: 21, 100; Fromm, 1955: 188, 241, 242; Russell, 1955: 225; Schweitzer, 1955: 202; Ponsoye, 1957: 101; Tournier, 1957: 20, 48, 78, 83, 91, 92, 98, 103; Whitehead, 1959: 107; Baur, 1960: 631; Bryson, 1960: 41, 42; Bryson, 1960a: 90, 91, 92; Bryson, 1960b: 643; Faust, 1960: 668; Maskin, 1960: 92, 93; Norman, 1960: 81, 110, 113; Schlesinger, 1960: 466, 477; Sinnott, 1960: 54; Wolff, 1960: 43, 72; Merton, 1961: 59, 60, 61; Rogers, 1961: 35, 108, 111; Kierkegaard, 1961: 110; Grabo, 1962: vi; Maslow, 1962: 5; Montagu, 1962: 11, 12, 156, 157; Parnes and Harding, 1962: vii; Murphy, 1963: 19, 114, 138, 139, 142; de Chardin, 1964: 61, 72, 118, 123, 185, 186, 187, 194, 195, 205, 207, 265, 266; Children's School, 1964: 211; Krishnamurti, 1964: 52; Bronowski, 1965: 10, 45, 51, 72; Weaver, 1965: 19, 52; Cobb, 1967: 97; Laotsu, 1967: 27; Moustakas, 1967: 92, 133; Spalding, 1967: 15; Allport, 1968: 406; Maslow, 1968: 153, 155, 193; Seifert, 1968: 23, 87, 155; Welk, 1968: 48, 49, 61, 62, 82, 83, 98; Gardner, 1969: 52, 60, 61, 64, 65, 105, 114, 115, 116, 132, 152, 160; Holmes, 1969: 120; May, 1969: 97, 242-243; Rogers, 1969: 190, 222, 227, 229, 233, 269, 274, 275; Carnegie, 1970: 78, 104, 119; Davis, 1970: 359; Freud, 1970: 78; Jung, 1970: 279, 282; Fromm, 1970: 325; Mailer, 1970: 382; McLuhan, 1970: 1; Pritzkau, 1970: 121; Reich, 1970: 174; Spivey, 1970: 344, 348; Weiss, 1970: 294; 296, 297; Bryson, 1971: 33; Gardner, 1971: 11, 121, 123,125, 127; Jourard, 1971: 6, 62, 113, 143, 178; Maslow, 1971b: 25; McConnell, 1971: 18, 77; O'Connor, 1971: 12, 83, 85; Maslow, 1971: 25; Novak, 1971: 47, 62; Peterson, 1971: 202; Buhler and Allen, 1972: 44; Eckstein, 1972: 1; Freire, 1972: 76, 77; 14; Laszlo, 1972: 109; Davidson, 1974: 325, 373; Dubos, 1974: 124; Forem, 1974: 2, 14, 19, 21, 23, 25, 29, 36, 37, 39, 75, 76, 99-100, 104, 122, 123, 161, 162, 172, 173, 174, 177, 178, 179, 225, 227, 237, 228; Huxley, 1974: 21; Maharishi Mahesh Yogi, 1974: 99; Mettler, 1974: 33, 55, 63, 71, 113; Millikan, 1974: 99; Bloomfield et al., 1975: 8, 145, 165, 189; Briggs, 1975: 113; Henderson, 1975: 3, 38, 45, 46, 98, 146, 147, 177; Koestler, 1975: 363-364; Roszak, 1975: 8, 9; Schuller, 1975: 141, 142; Schumacher, 1975: 153, 157, 277-278, 297; Arieti, 1976: 5, 13, 31; May, 1976: 55; Powell, 1976: 19, 20, 21, 23, 25, 26, 67, 82, 145, 158, 172, 176, 177; Toynbee, 1976: 361; Gramsci, 1977: 11; Howe, 1977: 29, 66, 83, 103, back; James and Jongeward, 1977: 158; Goldstein, 1978: 249,

250; Hall and Lindzey, 1978: 7, 21; Rogers, 1978: 7, 8; Rogers, 1979: 42; Torrance, 1979: 9; Bossart, 1980: 78, 91, 107, 223; Fox, 1980: 50, 81, 101, 102, 104, 107-108, 118, 129, 130, 131, 152, 160, 165, 231, 244, 249, 250, 252, 253, 254, 256, 260, 261, jacket; Krishnamurti, 1980: 11; Petacchi, 1980: 47, 51, 108; Sale, 1980: 157; Stevenson, 1980: 142; Elgin, 1981: 165; Freud, 1981: 228; Heilbroner, 1981: 189; Highet, 1981: 89, 90; Ross, 1981: 54, 106, 117, 150, 155, 173; Schaeffer, 1981: 116; Singer, 1981: 179; Theobald, 1981: 50, 144; Browning, 1982: 69; Buscaglia, 1982: 17, 21, 89, 91, 92, 110, 210; Young, 1982: 44; Capra, 1983: 358, 370, 371; Stuart, 1983: 54, 55, 58, 61; Swindoll, 1983: 216; Allport, 1984: 9, 10; Ash, 1984: 149; Bűhler, 1984: 146; Frankl, 1984: 87, 93-94, 101, 104, 105, 106, 113, 114, 115, 116, 121, 122, 131, 132, 141, 143, 144, 146, 147, 154, 169; Harman and Rheingold, 1984: xxii, 2, 7, 201; Lorenz, 1984: 146; Viscott, 1984: 151; Universal House of Justice, 1985: 2, 11; Bookchin, 1986: 13, 35; Buchholz and Roth, 1987: 149; Eyre, 1987: 10, 100, 135; Fuller, 1987: 131; Gide, 1987: 34; Kushner, 1987: 18, 19, 29, 33, 49, 69, 112, 117, 128, 140, 139, 141, 145, 150, 151, 160, 169, 172, 178, 179, back; MacAllister, 1987: 97; Sheehan, 1987: 96; Andrew, 1988: 49, back; Etzioni, 1988: 181; Ferencz and Keys, Jr., 1988: 34, 124; Paulson et al., 1988: 81, 201, 335; Amabile, 1989: ix, 7, 54, 116; Aquinas, 1989: 453; Beckman, 1989: 52; Jordan, 1989: 23; Klee, 1989: 52; Murphy, 1989: 92; Ray and Myers, 1989: 117, 127, 128, 130, 131; Shallcross and Sisk: 1989: xiv, 1, 87, 88, 91, 101; Sitwell, 1989: 52; Todaro, 1989: 89; Tulku, 1989: 201; Amos, 1990: 69; Briggs, 1990: 9, back; Covey, 1990: 147, 157, 171, 299, 304; Harman and Hormann, 1990: 26, 56, 61-62, 71, 82, 85, 90, 139; Jampolsky, 1990: v, 3, 4, 156, 202, back; Janger and Edmondson, 1990: 166; Maccoby, 1990: 94; Polanyi, 1990: 1; Scott-Bader, 1990: 146; Spencer, 1990: 166; Zukav, 1990: 13, 91, 122, 127, 128, 147, 159; Cliett, 1991: 280; Covey, 1991: 304; Csikszentmihalyi, 1991: 214, 215, 217; 218, 226, 227, 234; Dreher, 1991: xiv, xv, 4, 10, 12, 13, 26, 29, 50, 76, 90, 98, 104, 106, 122, 124, 125, 135, 159, 160, 173, 185, 187, 189, 195, 196, 199, 200, 201, 203, 214, 215, 255, 262; Elkind, 1991: 235; Fritz, 1991: 180, 185, 189; Gordon, 1991: 370; Hammarskjöld, 1991: 183, 184; Heilbroner, 1991: 134, 142, 144, 148, 149, 150, 187, 189, 190; Hill, 1991: 12; Huxley, 1991: 352; Jacobs, 1991: 288, 289; Jung, 1991: 204; Kessler, 1991: 7; Klopp, 1991: 156; Lane, 1991: 75; Mead, 1991: 321; Pearson, 1991: 127, 130, 131, 165, 171; Richardson, 1991: 102; Riles, 1991: 173; Satin, 1991: 199; Smith, 1991: 187-188; Snyder, 1991: 304, 306; Wilson, 1991: 183, 186, 187; Carr, 1992: 123; Dass and Bush, 1992: xi, 5, 13, 139, 159, 162, 164, 170, 180, 183, 222, 232, 233, 236, 239, 241, 247; Earth Charter Commission, 1992: 1; Kiros, 1992: 117; Parnes, 1992:16; Renesch, 1992: ix; Schaef, 1992: 82, 131, 150, 203, 252; Wenger, 1992: 133;

Zinsser, 1992: 64; Andrews, 1993: vii; Brutoco, 1993: xiii, xiv; de Broglie, 1993: 207; Brutoco, 1993: xii; Collins and Porras, 1993: 83, 84; Dewey, 1993: 43; Drummond, 1993: 97, 98, 99, 101; Henderson, 1993: 270; Jaffe and Scott, 1993: 140; Kazimierz, 1993: 110; Land and Jarman, 1993: 24, 137, 139, 160, 177, 179-180, 186, 191, 193, 212, 221; Mandel, 1993: 166; Nirenberg, 1993: 2, 41, 53, 61; Peck, 1993: 11-12, 21, 23, 33, 61, 66, 68, 70, 78, 79, 112; Pinchot and Pinchot, 1993: 246, 247; Ray, 1993: 161; Rolland, 1993: 99; Schubert, 1993: 81; Vaclav, 1993: 186; Zukav, 1993: 240, 241; Acquinas, 1994: 164; Chopra, 1994: 3, 7, 95, 96, 97, 98; Cohen and Manion, 1994: 8; Covey, Merrill, and Merrill, 1994: 65, 95, 103, 105, 106, 110, 113, 131, 132, 145, 150, 151, 161, 219, 256; Csikszentmihalyi, 1994: xiv, xv, xvi, xvii, xviii, 5, 11-12, 17, 23, 29, 71, 77, 86, 153, 158, 162, 175, 176, 177, 178, 191, 196, 197, 201, 207, 208, 219, 221, 241, 242, 244, 246, 248, 249, 266, 269, 292; Eckhart, 1994: 116; Fox (Matthew) 1994: 2, 5, 6, 9, 10, 14, 15, 30, 32, 41, 47, 54, 55, 56, 61, 65, 69, 70, 71, 76, 81-82, 83, 87, 97-98, 100, 102, 103, 104, 110, 111, 112, 115, 116, 117, 119, 120, 127, 129, 142, 144, 161, 169, 180, 246; Fox (Warwick), 1994: 205; Grof, 1994: 202; Harvey and Matousek, 1994: 136, 137, 138, 146, 160, 165, 200; Heschel, 1994: 176; Jung, 1994: 120; Kasl, 1994: xv; 3; Mandela, 1994; Macy, 1994: 205, 206; Mayor, 1994: 200; Moore, 1994: 19, 20, 41, 45, 113, 117, 121, 122, 127, 143, 146, 179, 181, 184, 185, 199, 228, 237, 243, 255, 261, 274, 275, 288, 299, 300; Schumacher, 1994: 220; Terkel, 1994: 95; Chopra, 1995: 5, 6, 9; Dyer, 1995: 25, 26, 33, 41, 44, 45, 55, 57, 61, 62. Jones, 1995: v, xii, xiii, xiv, xv, 3, 46, 70, 71, 121, 122, 123, 140, 143, 162, 175, 177, 178, 179, 180, 181, 182, 183, 190, 193, 194, 195, 198; back; Neck, 1995: x, 3; Peck, 1995: 170; Swindoll, 1995: 499; Thiss, 1995: 82, 83, 84, 85, 100, 161, 169, jacket; Waitley, 1995: 13, 45, 46, 47, 52, 91, 94, 111, 131, 132, 134, 136, 137, 164, 170, 251; Benson, 1996: 15, 17, 24, 195, 196, 197, 199, 212, 213; Senge, 1995: i; Blackmore, 1996: 210; Csikszentmihalyi, 1996: 1, 182, 370, 371; Evans, 1996: 200, 266, 299; Hillman, 1996: 4, 5, 6, 10, 11, 40, 74, 85, 133, 134, 135, 136, 138, 139, 150, 171, 203, 234, 278, 285, jacket; Jung, 1996: x; Moore, 1996: 285, 313; Quinn, 1996: cover, xiv, 11, 25, 35, 37, 44, 46, 70, 148, 215; Siebert, 1996: 260; Bellman, 1997: 164; Bennis and Biederman, 1997: 198, 210; Collins and Porras, 1997: 82, 83, 84, 187, 219; Cayce, 1997: xi; Graham, 1997: 69, 70; Hesselbein, 1997: jacket; Keen, 1997: back; Leider, 1997: 1, 3, 4, 21, 24, 30, 31, 32, 33, 34, 35, 36, 38, 39, 51, 56, 60, 70, 77, 80, 81, 84, 89, 90, 91, 96, 118, 128, 129, 132, 133, 162; Leider and Shapiro, 1997: 164; Levoy, 1997: 4, 5, 7, 8,21, 35, 191, 209, 274, 279; Morse, 1997: 197; Mundale, 1997: back cover; Parnes, 1997: 55; Spady and Bell, 1997: 138; Thurston, 1997: iii, xxii, xxiii, xxiv, xxv, xxviii, 9, 11-12, 13, 15, 17, 32, 34, 35, 36, 42, 43, 44, 49, 51, 55, 59, 60, 61, 62, 66, 68, 69, 80, 84, 87, 91, 107, 108, 110, 111, 123, 165, 170, 171, 175, 176, 178, 184, back; Utne, 1997:

jacket; Wolf (Susan), 1997: 210, 211; Wolf (Naomi), 1997: 89; Bleedorn,1998: xvii, 3; Bolden et al., 1998: 6, 8, 25, 27, 53; Breathnach, 1998: iii, 3, 148; Chopra, 1998: 73, 112; Goater, 1998: xi; Hurston, 1998: 72; Hultman, 1998: 17; Le Guin, 1998: 60; Jung, 1998:301; Moore, 1998: 127; Moss, 1998: 61, 99, 105, 133, jacket; Robinson, 1998: 30; Sejnowski, 1998: 14, 15; Talku, 1998: 73; Toms and Toms, 1998: 5, 30, 75, 79, 81, 84, 87, 91, 98, 138, 164, 169, 178, 180, 188, 206; Berry, 1999: 7, 10, 14, 15, 18, 24, 118, 158, 160, 161, 163, 165, 167, 168, 173, 175; Blanchard, 1999: 103; Buber, 1999: 24; Childre and Martin, 1999: 51, 177, 237, 259; Gibson, 1999: 137, Jaccaci and Gault, 1999: 77, 119; Loeb, 1999: 135, 138, 160; Martin, 1999: xvii; Pohle and Selover, 1999: 151; Richmond, 1999: 5, 111, 112, 113, 117, 119, 121, 132, 133, 135, 139, 140, 153; Sirolli, 1999: 18; Bockl, 2000: 49, 64, 71, 112; Eckert and Vehar, 2000: 24, 45, 78, 87; Jaccaci, 2000: 34, 68; Nelson, 2000: 77; Paine, 2000: 177; Ray and Anderson, 2000: 73, 345, 346; Rousseau, 2000, vii; White, 2001: 155, 157, 159, 174; Debold, 2002: 58, 63; Eisler, 2002: xi, 62, 170, 181, 182, 186, 198, 200; Spady and Kirby, 2002: 178; Cohen, 2003: 83; Crème, 2003: 115; Dalai Lama and Cutler, 2003: 70, 77, 79, 184; Desjardins, 2003: 107; Dichter, 2003: 162; Dolnick, 2003: 3, 4, 23; Hamilton, 2003: 101; Harding, 2003: 102; Long, 2003: 117; Mapes, 2003: 78, 110, 114, 185, 186, 188, 197, 198, 199, 200; Senge, 2003: 50; Swimme, 2003: 43; Anderson, 2004: 147, 275, 284; Burton, 2004: 237, 243; Emoto, 2004: 98; Henderson, 2004: 13, 16, 17, 21, 22, 28, 32, 39, 83, 98, 101, 127, 163; Ikeda, 2004: 13, 15, 16, 17, 24, 40, 54, 55, 82, 83, 101, 123, 124, 150, 153, 158; Lombardo and Richter, 2004: 280; Orr, 2004: 104, 105, 108, 111; Schweitzer, 2004: 177; Secretan, 2004: 58, 59, 84, 85, 123, 125, 130; Stewart, 2004: 284; Wenger, 2004; Gardner, 2005: 59; Lee, 2005: 13, 19, 20, 21, 99, 100, 102, 105, 106, 107, 110, 111, 112, 114, 118, 119, 120, 121, 173, 180; May, 2005: 59; McDowell, 2005:1; Siebert, 2005: 191-192; Walsch, 2005: 11; Wright, 2005: 47, 48, 51, 169, 170, 172, 177; Gilles, 2006: 106, 119, 128, 139, 141, 148, 149, 151, 169, 195; Chryssomallis, 2007; Alexander, 2008; Fox, 2008; George et al., 2008; Jaccaci, 2008: 1; Jefferson and Jaccaci, 2008: i, 20, 21, 24, 34, 41, 42; Newell, 2008; Kristina, 2009; Ryan, 2009; Yunus with Weber, 2010: 27, 28; Gangadean, 2012; Schrödinger, 2012.

References

Alexander, Elizabeth, 2008.
Radio Interview, National Public Radio, *All Things Considered,* December 18. http://www.npr.org/templates/story/story.php?storyId=98467631.

Allport, Gordon, 1955.
Becoming: Basic Considerations for a Psychology of Personality. (New Haven: Yale University Press).

Allport, Gordon, 1968.
The Person in Psychology. (Boston: Beacon Press).

Allport, Gordon, 1984.
"Preface." In Viktor Frankl, *Man's Search for Meaning.* Revised and Updated. (New York: Washington Square Press).

Amabile, Teresa M., 1989.
Growing Up Creative: Nurturing a Lifetime of Creativity. (New York: Crown Publishers, Inc.).

Amos, Wally, 1990.
Quoted is Gerald G. Jampolsky, *One Person Can Make a Difference: Ordinary People Doing Extraordinary Things.* (New York: Bantam Books).

Anderson, Nancy, 2004.
Work with Passion: How to Do What You Love for a Living. Revised and expanded. (Novato, California: New World Library).

Anderson, Walter Truett, 2004.
Quoted in Thomas Lombardo and Jonathan Richter, "Evolving Future Consciousness Through the Pursuit of Virtue." In Howard F. Didsbury Jr. and the Staff of the World Future Society (eds.), *Thinking Creatively in Turbulent Times.* (Bethesda, Maryland: World Future Society), pp. 257-288.

Andrew, Brother with Dave and Neta Jackson, 1988.
A Time for Heroes. (Ann Arbor, Michigan: Servant Publications).

Andrews, Robert, 1993.
"Introduction." In Robert Andrews (ed.), *The Columbia Dictionary of Quotations.* (New York: Columbia University Press), pp. vii-x.

Aquinas, St. Thomas, 1989.
Summa Theologiae: A Concise Translation, Timothy McDernott (ed.). (London: Eyre & Spottiswoode).

Aquinas, Thomas, 1994.
Quoted in Matthew Fox, *The Reinvention of Work: A New Vision of Livelihood for Our Time.* (New York: HarperCollins Publishers).

Arieti, Silvano, 1976.
Creativity: The Magic Synthesis. (New York: Basic Books, Inc.).

Ash, Mary Kay, 1984.
Mary Kay on People Management. (New York: Warner Books, Inc.).

Baur, John I. H., 1960.
"Painting and Sculpture." In Lyman Bryson (ed.), *An Outline of Man's Knowledge of the Modern World.* (New York: Nelson Doubleday, Inc.), pp. 619-631.

Beckman, Max, 1989.
Quoted in Doris J. Shallcross and Dorothy A. Sisk, *Intuition: An Inner Way of Knowing.* (Buffalo, New York: Bearly Limited).

Bellman, Geoffrey M., 1997.
Your Signature Path. Book description. In Richard J. Leider, *The Power of Purpose: Creating Meaning in Your Life and Work.* (San Francisco: Berrett-Koehler Publishers, Inc.).

Bennis, Warren and Patricia Ward Biederman, 1997.
Organizing Genius: The Secrets of Creative Collaboration. (Reading, Massachusetts: Addison-Wesley Publishing Company, Inc.).

Benson, Herbert with Marg Stark, 1996.
Timeless Healing: The Power and Biology of Belief. (New York: Scribner).

Berry, Thomas, 1999.
The Great Work: Our Way Into the Future. (New York: Bell Tower).

Blackmore, S. 1996.
Dying to Live: Near-Death Experiences. (Buffalo, New York: Prometheus Books, 1993). Quoted in Herbert Benson with Marg Stark, *Timeless Healing: The Power and Biology of Belief.* (New York: Scribner).

Blanchard, Ken, 1999.
The Heart of a Leader: Insights on the Art of Leading. (Tulsa, Oklahoma: Honor Books).

Bleedorn, Berenice, 1998.
The Creativity Force in Education, Business, and Beyond: An Urgent Message. (Lakeville, Minnesota: Galde Press, Inc.).

Bloomfield, Harold H. et al, 1975.
Transcendental Meditation: Discovering Inner Energy and Overcoming Stress. (New York: Delacorte Press).

Bockl, George, 2000.
Where Did We Come From and Where Are We Going? In Search of a Road to Universal Spirituality. First Edition. (Marina del Ray, California: DeVorss Publications).

Bolden, Vernie, Raymond F. Paloutzian, and Robert V. Guthrie, 1998.
An Integration of Psychology, Philosophy, Psychiatry, and Religion: Personalities and Events. Second Edition. (Boston: Allyn and Bacon).

Bookchin, Murray, 1986.
The Modern Crisis. (Philadelphia: New Society Publishers).

Bossart, Donald, 1980.
Creative Conflict in Religious Education and Church Administration. (Birmingham, Alabama: Religious Education Press).

Breathnach, Sarah Ban, 1998.
Something More: Excavating Your Authentic Self. (New York: Warner Books, Inc.).

Briggs, Dorothy Corkille, 1975.
Your Child's Self-Esteem: Step-by-Step Guidelines for Raising Responsible, Productive, Happy Children. Dolphin Books Edition. (New York: Doubleday and Company, Inc.).

Briggs, John, 1990.
Fire in the Crucible: The Self-Creation of Creativity and Genius. (Los Angeles: Jeremy P. Tarcher, Inc.).

Bronowski, Jacob, 1965.
Science and Human Values. (New York: Harper and Row, Publishers).

Browning, Robert, 1982.
"Paracelsus." Quoted in George & Vaune Ainsworth-Land, *Forward to Basics.* (Buffalo, New York: D. O. K. Publishers).

Brutoco, Rinaldo S., 1993.
"Foreword: Sculpting a New Business Paradigm." In Michael Ray and Alan Rinzler (eds.), *The New Paradigm in Business: Emerging Strategies for Leadership and Organizational Change.* (New York: Jeremy P. Tarcher), pp. xi - xiv.

Bryson, Lyman, 1960.
Introduction to Harold G. Wolff, "The Mind-Body Relationship." In Lyman Bryson (ed.), *An Outline of Man's Knowledge of the Modern World.* (New York: Nelson Doubleday, Inc.), pp. 41-72.

Bryson, Lyman, 1960a.
Introduction to Meyer Maskin, "The Science of Personality." In Lyman Bryson (ed.), *An Outline of Man's Knowledge of the Modern World.* (New York: Nelson Doubleday, Inc.), pp. 90-92.

Bryson, Lyman, 1960b.
Introduction to Ernest Nagel, "The Mission of Philosophy." In Lyman Bryson (ed.), *An Outline of Man's Knowledge of the Modern World.* (New York: Nelson Doubleday, Inc.), pp. 643-646.

Bryson, Lyman, 1971.
Quoted in John W. Gardner, *Self-Renewal: The Individual and the Innovative Society.* Perennial Library. (New York: Harper & Row, Publishers).

Buber, Martin, 1999.
Martin Buber on Psychology and psychotherapy. Essays, Letters, and Dialogue. Edited by Judith Buber Agassi. (Syracuse, New York: Syracuse University Press).

Buchholz Steve and Thomas Roth, 1987.
Creating the High-Performance Team. (New York: John Wiley & Sons, Inc.).

Bűhler, Charlotte, 1984.
"Basic Theoretical Concepts of Humanistic Psychology," *American Psychologist,* XXVI, April. Quoted in Viktor Frankl, *Man's Search for Meaning: An Introduction to Logotherapy.* Touchstone Edition. (New York: Simon & Schuster).

Bűhler, Charlotte, and Melanie Allen, 1972.
Introduction to Humanistic Psychology. (Belmont, California: Brooks/Cole Publishing Company).

Burton, Lynn Elen, 2004.
"Creativity, Innovation, and Visionary Thinking: Becoming All You Can Become." In Howard F. Didsbury Jr. and the Staff of the World Future Society (eds.), *Thinking Creatively in Turbulent Times.* (Bethesda, Maryland: World Future Society), pp. 236-244.

Buscaglia, Leo F., 1982.
Personhood: The Art of Being Fully Human. First Ballantine Books Edition. (New York: Ballantine Books).

Cayce, Charles Thomas, 1997.
"Foreword." In Mark Thurston, *Soul Purpose: Discovering and Fulfilling Your Destiny.* (New York: St. Martin's Press), pp. ix-xi.

Capra, Fritjof, 1983.
The Turning Point: Science, Society, and the Rising Culture. (Toronto: Bantam Books).

Carnegie, Dale, 1970.
How to Enjoy Your Life and Your Job. (New York: Simon and Schuster).

Carr, Clay, 1992.
Smart Training: The Manager's Guide to Training for Improved Performance. (New York: McGraw-Hill, Inc.).

Channing, William Ellery, 1993.
Quoted in Dan Millman, *The Life You Were Born to Live: A Guide to Finding Your Life Purpose.* (Tiburon, California: H. J. Kramer, Inc.).

Childre, Doc and Howard Martin, 2000.
The Heartmath Solution. First HarperCollins Paperback Edition. (New York: HarperCollins Publishers, Inc.).

Children's School, 1964.
Quoted in Lawrence A Cremin, *The Transformation of the School: Progressivism in American Education 1876-1957.* (New York: Vintage Books).

Chopra, Deepak, 1994.
The Seven Laws of Spiritual Success: A Practical Guide to the Fulfillment of Your Dreams. (San-Rafael, California: Amber-Allen Publishing) .

Chopra, Deepak, 1995.
The Way of the Wizard: Twenty Spiritual Lessons for Creating the Life You Want. (New York: Harmony Books).

Chopra, Deepak, 1998.
Quoted in Michael Toms and Justine Willis Toms, *True Work.* (New York: Bell Tower).

Chryssomallis, Yannis, 2007.
"Tribute." Life Performance, The Taj Mahal, September 13.

Cliett, Bill Cole, 1991.
"Sylvia Ashton-Warner's Message for American Teachers." In James D. Quisenberry, E. Anne Eddowes, and Sandra L. Robinson (eds.), *Readings from Childhood Education,* Volume II. (Wheaton, Maryland: Association for Childhood Education International), pp. 279-280.

Cobb, Stanwood, 1967.
The Importance of Creativity. (Metuchen, New Jersey: The Scarecrow Press, Inc.).

Cohen, Andrew, 2003.
"Exploring the Future of Religion: Andrew Cohen and Ken Wilber in Dialogue," *What is Enlightenment? Wake Up to a New World,* Spring/Summer, pp. 83-93.

Cohen, Louis and Lawrence Manion, 1994.
Research Methods in Education. Fourth Edition. (London: Routledge).

Collins, James C. and Jerry I. Porras, 1993.
"Purpose, Mission, and Vision." In Michael Ray and Alan Rinzler (eds.), *The New Paradigm in Business: Emerging Strategies for Leadership and Organizational Change.* (New York: Jeremy P. Tarcher), pp. 82 - 89.

Collins, James C., and Jerry I. Porras, 1997.
Built to Last: Successful Habits of Visionary Companies. First Paperback Edition. (New York: HarperBusiness).

Covey, Stephen R., 1990.
The 7 Habits of Highly Effective People: Powerful Lessons in Personal Change. First Fireside Edition. (New York: Simon & Schuster).

Covey, Stephen R., 1991.
Principle-Centered Leadership. (New York: Simon & Schuster).

Covey, Stephen R., A. Roger Merrill, and Rebecca R. Merrill, 1994.
First Things First: To Live, to Love, and to Leave a Legacy. (New York: Simon and Schuster).

Crème, Benjamin, 2003.
(Book Announcement.) In *What is Enlightenment? Wake Up to a New World,* Spring/Summer, p. 115.

Csikszentmihalyi, Mihaly, 1991.
Flow: The Psychology of Optimal Experience. First HarperPerennial Edition. (New York: Harper Collins Publishers).

Csikszentmihalyi, Mihaly, 1994.
The Evolving Self: A Psychology for the Third Millennium. First HarperPerennial Edition. (New York: Harper Collins Publishers).

Csikszentmihalyi, Mihaly, 1996.
Creativity: Flow and the Psychology of Discovery and Invention. (New York: Harper Collins Publishers).

Dalai Lama (The), His Holiness and Howard C. Cutler, 2003.
The Art of Happiness at Work. (New York: Riverside Books).

Dass, Ram and Mirabai Bush, 1992.
Compassion in Action: Setting Out on the path of Service. (New York: Bell Tower).

Davidson, Robert F., 1974.
Philosophies Men Live By. Second Edition. (New York: Holt, Rinehart and Winston, Inc.).

Davis, Joseph K., 1970.
"The Crisis of Identity." In Joseph K. Davis (ed.), *Man in Crisis: Perspectives on the Individual and His World.* (Glenview, Illinois: Scott, Foresman and Company), pp. 357-360.

de Broglie, Louis, 1993.
Quoted in George Land and Beth Jarman, *Breakpoint and Beyond: Mastering the Future – Today.* First Paperback Edition. (New York: HarperCollins Publishers, Inc.).

de Chardin, Pierre Teilhard, 1964.
The Future of Man. (New York, Harper & Row, Publishers).

Debold, Elizabeth, 2002.
"Boomeritis & Me: Not Just a Book Review." In *What is Enlightenment? Wake Up to a New World,* Fall/Winter, pp. 55-63.

Desjardins, Arnaud, 2003.
(Interview.) In *What is Enlightenment? Wake Up to a New World,* Spring/Summer, p. 107.

Dewey, John, 1993.

Quoted in Dale Carnegie & Associates, Inc., *The Leader in You: How to Win Friends, Influence People and Succeed in a Changing World.* (New York: Pocket Books).

Dichter, Thomas W., 2003.

Despite Good Intentions: Why Development Assistance in The Third World Has Failed. (Amherst & Boston: University of Massachusetts Press).

Dolnick, Barrie, 2003.

Minerva Rules Your Future: Goddess-Given Advice for Smart Moves at Work. (New York: Harmony Books).

Dreher, Diane, 1991.

The Tao of Inner Peace. First HarperPerennial Edition. (New York: HarperPerennial).

Drummond, Henry, 1993.

The Greatest Thing in the World. (Uhrichsville, Ohio: Barbour and Company, Inc.).

Dubos, René, 1974.

"Can Man Adapt to Megalopolis," *The Ecologist,* January 1970. Quoted in Edward Goldsmith, *et al.*, 1974. *Blueprint for Survival.* First Signet Printing. (New York: The New American Library, Inc.).

Dyer, Wayne W., 1995.

Your Sacred Self: Making the Decision to be Free. (New York: HarperCollins Publishers).

Earth Charter Commission, 1992.

The Earth Charter. http://www.earthcharterinaction.org/invent/images/uploads/echarter_english.pdf.

Eckert, Bob and Jonathan Vehar, 2000.

More Lightening Less Thunder: How to Energize Innovation Teams. (Lake Placid, New York: New and Improved).

Eckhart, Meister, 1994.
Quoted in Matthew Fox, *The Reinvention of Work: A New Vision of Livelihood for Our Time.* (New York: HarperCollins Publishers).

Eckstein, George R., 1972.
"Pleasure for the Creative Mind." In Angelo M. Biondi (ed.), *The Creative Process.* (Buffalo, New York: D. O. K. Publishers).

Einstein, Albert, 1954.
"*Ideas and Opinions.* Collected Writings. (New York: Bonanza Books, 1954).

Eisler, Riane, 2002.
The Power of Partnership: Seven Relationships That Will Change Your Life. (Novato, California: New World Library).

Elgin, Duane, 1981.
Voluntary Simplicity: Toward a Way of Life That is Outwardly Simple, Inwardly Rich. (New York: William Morrow & Company).

Elgin, Duane, 1999.
"Traditional Western View of Reality." In Michael Schut *et al* (eds.), *Simpler Living: Compassionate Life.* (Denver, Colorado: Living the Good News, 1999), pp. 194-196.

Elkind, David, 1991.
"Humanizing the Curriculum." In James D. Quisenberry, E. Anne Eddowes, and Sandra L. Robinson (eds.), *Readings from Childhood Education,* Volume II. (Wheaton, Maryland: Association for Childhood Education International), pp. 235-241.

Emoto, Masaru, 2004.
The Hidden Messages in Water. (New York: Atria Books).

Etzioni, Amitai, 1988.
The Moral Dimension: Toward a New Economics. (New York: The Free Press).

Evans, Robert, 1996.
The Human Side of School Change: Reform, Resistance, and the Real-Life Problems of Innovation. (San Francisco: Jossey-Brass Publishers).

Eyre, Stephen D., 1987.
Defeating the Dragons of the World: Resisting the Seduction of False Values. (Downers Grove, Illinois: InterVarsity Press).

Faust, Clarence, H., 1960.
"The Search for Answers." In Lyman Bryson (ed.), *An Outline of Man's Knowledge of the Modern World.* (New York: Nelson Doubleday, Inc.), pp. 667-677.

Ferencz, Benjamin B. and Ken Keyes, Jr., 1988.
PlanetHood: The Key to Your Survival and Prosperity. (Coos Bay, Oregon: Vision Books).

Forem, Jack, 1974.
Transcendental Meditation: Maharishi Mahesh Yogi and the Science of Creative Intelligence. (New York: E. P. Dutton & Co., Inc.).

Fox, James. 2008.
"Natural Law." In *The Catholic Encyclopedia,* Vol. 9. (New York: Robert Appleton Company, 1910). Retrieved December 22, 2008 from New Advent: http://www.newadvent.org/cathen/09076a.htm.

Fox, Matthew, 1994.
The Reinvention of Work: A New Vision of Livelihood for Our Time. (New York: HarperCollins Publishers).

Fox, Michael, 1980.
One Earth, One Mind: Personal Notes Toward a New Natural Consciousness. (New York: Coward, McCann, and Geoghegan).

Fox, Warwick, 1994.
Quoted in Matthew Fox, *The Reinvention of Work: A New Vision of Livelihood for Our Time.* (New York: HarperCollins Publishers).

Frankl, Viktor Emil, 1984.
Man's Search for Meaning: An Introduction to Logotherapy. Third Edition. A Touchstone Book. (New York: Simon & Schuster).

Frankl, Viktor E., 1994.
Quoted in Stephen R. Covey, A. Roger Merrill and Rebecca R. Merrill, *First Things First: To Live, to Love, to Learn, to Leave a Legacy.* (New York: Simon and Schuster).

Freire, Paulo, 1972.
Pedagogy of the Oppressed. (London: Sheed and Ward Ltd.).

Freud, Sigmund, 1970.
Quoted in Dale Carnegie, *How to Enjoy Your Life and Your Job.* (New York: Simon and Schuster).

Freud, Sigmund, 1981.
Quoted in Robert L, Heilbroner, "How to Make an Intelligent Decision." In Reader's Digest (ed.), *Mind Power: How to Develop It ... Use It ... Expand It!* (New York: Berkley Books), pp. 226-229.

Fritz, Robert, 1991.
Creating. (New York: Fawcett Columbine).

Fromm, Erich, 1955.
The Sane Society. (New York: Fawcett World Library).

Fromm, Erich, 1970.
"Love and Its Disintegration in Contemporary Western Society." In Joseph K. Davis (ed.), *Man in Crisis: Perspectives on the Individual and His World.* (Glenview, Illinois: Scott, Foresman and Company), pp. 323-335.

Fuller, Margaret, 1987.
Woman in the Nineteenth Century: A Facsimile of the 1845 Edition. Edited by Joel Myerson and Introduced by Madeline B. Stern. (Columbis, South Carolina: University of South Carolina Press, 1980), p. 26. Quoted in Jeffrey Steele, *The Representation of the Self in the American Renaissance.* (Chapel Hill, North Carolina: The University of North Carolina Press, 1987).

Gangadean, Ashok K., 2012.
http://www.awakeningmind.org/pages/agcarticle.php.

Gardncr, John W., 1969.
No Easy Victories. First Harper Colophon Edition. (New York: Harper and Row Publishers).

Gardner, John W., 1971.
Self-Renewal: The Individual and the Innovative Society. Perennial Library. (New York: Harper & Row, Publishers).

Gardner, John W., 2005.
Quoted in Vinita Hampton Wright, *The Soul Tells a Story: Engaging Creativity with Spirituality in the Writing Life.* (Downers Grove, Illinois: InterVarsity Press).

Gender Coaches, 2009.
www.gendercoaches.com/global-consciousness-petition

George, Bill, Andrew McLean, and Nick Craig, 2008.
Finding Your True North: A Personal Guide. (New York: Harvard Business School Press).

Gibson, William, 1999.
"The Lifestyle of Christian Faithfulness." In Michael Schut *et al.,* (eds.), *Simpler Living: Compassionate Life.* (Denver, Colorado: Living the Good News, 1999), pp. 131-139.

Gide, Andre, 1987.
Quoted in Marsha Sinetar, *Do What You Love, The Money Will Follow: Discovering Your Right Livelihood.* (New York: Dell Publishing).

Gilles, Barbara Ray, 2006.
Nurturing Civilization Builders: Birthing the Best Schools in the World. (Seattle: Oak Forest Press).

Goater, Gill, 1998.
Words That Shine Both Ways. (Oakhurst, California: Enneas Publications).

Goldstein, Kurt 1978.
The Organism. (New York: American Book Company, 1939). Reviewed in Calvin S. Hall and Gardner Lindzey, *Theories of Personality.* Third Edition. (New York: John Wiley & Sons, Inc.).

Goldstein, Kurt, 2011.
The Organism: A Holistic Approach to Biology Derived from Pathological Data in Man.
http://en.wikipedia.org/wiki/Self_actualized#Self-actualization_in_Goldstein.27s_Theory

Gordon, Ira. J., 1991.
"Nurturing Our Roots." In James D. Quisenberry, E. Anne Eddowes, and Sandra L. Robinson (eds.), *Readings from Childhood Education,* Volume II. (Wheaton, Maryland: Association for Childhood Education International), pp. 370-379.

Gozdz, Kazimierz, 1993.
"Building Community as Leadership Discipline." In Michael Ray and Alan Rinzler (eds.), *The New Paradigm in Business: Emerging Strategies for Leadership and Organizational Change.* (New York: Jeremy P. Tarcher), pp. 107 - 119.

Grabo, Carl H., 1962.
Quoted in Sidney J. Parnes and Harold F. Harding "Preface." In Sidney J. Parnes and Harold F. Harding, (eds.), *A Source Book for Creative Thinking.* (New York: Charles Scribner's Sons).

Graham, Stedman, 1997.
You Can Make It happen: A Nine-Step Plan for Success. (New York: Simon & Schuster).

Gramsci, Antonio, 1977.
Selections from Political Writings: 1910-20. Edited by Quintin Hoare. (New York: International Publishers).

Grof, Stanislav, 1994.
Quoted in Matthew Fox, *The Reinvention of Work: A New Vision of Livelihood for Our Time.* (New York: HarperCollins Publishers).

Hall, Calvin S. and Gardner Lindzey, 1978.
Theories of Personality. Third Edition. (New York: John Wiley & Sons, Inc.).

Hamilton, Craig, 2003.
(Interview.) In *What is Enlightenment? Wake Up to a New World,* Spring/Summer, p. 101.

Hammarskjöld, Dag, 1991.
Markings. (New York: Alfred A. Knopf, Inc., 1965), pp. 13, 157. Quoted in Diane Dreher, *The Tao of Inner Peace.* First HarperPerennial Edition. (New York: HarperPerennial).

Harding, Douglas, 2003.
(Interview.) In *What is Enlightenment? Wake Up to a New World,* Spring/Summer, p. 102.

Harman, Willis and Howard Rheingold, 1984.
Higher Creativity: Liberating the Unconscious for Breakthrough Insights. (Los Angeles, California: Jeremy Tharcher, Inc.).

Harman, Willis and John Hormann, 1990.
Creative Work: The Constructive Role of Business in a Transforming Society.(Indianapolis, Indiana: Knowledge Systems, Inc.).

Harvey, Andrew and Mark Matousek, 1994.
Dialogues with a Modern Mystic. (Wheaton, Illinois: The Theosophical Publishing House).

Heilbroner, Robert L., 1981.
"How to Make an Intelligent Decision." In Reader's Digest (ed.), *Mind Power: How to Develop It ... Use It ... Expand It!* (New York: Berkley Books), pp. 226-229.

Heilbroner, Robert L., 1991.
An Inquiry into the Human Prospect: Looked at Again for the 1990s. (New York: W. W. Norton and Company, Inc.).

Henderson, C. William, 1975.
Awakening: Ways to Psycho-Spiritual Growth. (Englewood Cliffs, New Jersey: Prentice Hall, Inc.).

Henderson, Hazel, 1993.

"The Age of Light." In Michael Ray and Alan Rinzler (eds.), *The New Paradigm in Business: Emerging Strategies for Leadership and Organizational Change.* (New York: Jeremy P. Tarcher), pp. 267-275.

Henderson, Hazel, 2004.

In Hazel Henderson and Daisaku Ikeda. *Planetary Citizenship: Your Values, Beliefs, and Actions Can Shape a Sustainable Future.* (Santa Monica, California: Middleway Press).

Heschel, Rabbi Abraham, 1994.

Quoted in Matthew Fox, *The Reinvention of Work: A New Vision of Livelihood for Our Time.* (New York: HarperCollins Publishers).

Hesselbein, Frances, 1997.

(Book Endorsement.) Richard J. Leider, *The Power of Purpose: Creating Meaning in Your Life and Work.* (San Francisco: Berrett-Koehler Publishers, Inc.).

Highet, Gilbert, 1981.

"Man's Unconquerable Mind." In Reader's Digest (ed.), *Mind Power: How to Develop It ... Use It ... Expand It!* (New York: Berkley Books), pp. 84-90.

Hill, Patty Smith, 1991.

Quoted in Mary Anne Fowlkes, "Gifts from Childhood's Godmother – Patty Smith Hill." In James D. Quisenberry, E. Anne Eddowes, and Sandra L. Robinson (eds.), *Readings from Childhood Education,* Volume II. (Wheaton, Maryland: Association for Childhood Education International), pp. 11-15.

Hillman, James, 1996.

The Soul's Code: In Search of Character and Calling. (New York: Random House, Inc.).

Holmes, Arthur F., 1969.

Christian Philosophy in the Twentieth Century: An Essay in Philosophical Methodology. (Nutley, New Jersey: The Craig Press).

Holmes, Ernest, 1950.
How to Use the Science of Mind. (New York: G. P. Putnam's Sons).

Howe, Reuel L., 1977.
Live All Your Life. Third Paperback Printing (Waco, Texas: Word Books, Publisher).

Hultman, Ken, 1998.
Making Change Irresistible: Overcoming Resistance to Change in Your Organization. (Palo Alto, California: Davies-Black Publishers).

Hurston, Zora Neale, 1998.
Quotted in Sarah Ban Breathnach, *Something More: Excavating Your Authentic Self.* (New York: Warner Books, Inc.).

Huxley, Julian, 1974.
Quoted in Jack Forem, *Transcendental Meditation: Maharishi Mahesh Yogi and the Science of Creative Intelligence.* (New York: E. P. Dutton & Co., Inc.).

Huxley, Julian (Sir), 1991.
Quoted in Stewart L. Udall, "Ecological Balance." In James D. Quisenberry, E. Anne Eddowes, and Sandra L. Robinson (eds.), *Readings from Childhood Education,* Volume II. (Wheaton, Maryland: Association for Childhood Education International), pp. 351-353.

Ikeda, Daisaku, 2004.
In Hazel Henderson and Daisaku Ikeda.*Planetary Citizenship: Your Values, Beliefs, and Actions Can Shape a Sustainable Future.* (Santa Monica, California: Middleway Press).

Jaccaci, August T. and Susan B. Gault, 1999.
Chief Evolutionary Officer: Leaders Mapping the Future. (Boston, Massachusetts: Butterworth-Heinemann).

Jaccaci, August T., 2000.
General Periodicity: Nature's Creative Dynamics. (Thetford Center, Vermont: Unity Scholars, Inc.).

Jaccaci, August T., 2008.
"Creating Communities: Partners in Whole Community Learning." COM'V 08 conference flyer. (New Gloucester, Maine: Unity Scholars).

Jacobs, Leland B., 1991.
"The Meaning of Teaching." In James D. Quisenberry, E. Anne Eddowes, and Sandra L. Robinson (eds.), *Readings from Childhood Education,* Volume II. (Wheaton, Maryland: Association for Childhood Education International), pp. 287-292.

Jaffe, Dennis T., and Cynthia D. Scott, 1993.
"Building a Committed Workplace: An Empowered Organization as a Competitive Advantage." In Michael Ray and Alan Rinzler (eds.), *The New Paradigm in Business: Emerging Strategies for Leadership and Organizational Change.* (New York: Jeremy P. Tarcher), pp. 139 - 146.

James, Muriel and Dorothy Jongeward, 1977.
Born to Win: Transactional Analysis with Gestalt Experiments. Thirty-seventh printing. (Reading, Massachusetts: Addison-Wesley Publishing Company).

Jampolsky, Gerald G., 1990.
One Person Can Make a Difference: Ordinary People Doing Extraordinary Things. (New York: Bantam Books).

Janger, Standford M. and Amy C. Edmondson, 1990.
"Business in Transformation." In Willis Harman and John Hormann, *Creative Work: The Constructive Role of Business in a Transforming Society.*(Indianapolis, Indiana: Knowledge Systems, Inc.), pp. 161 - 195.

Jefferson, Thomas and August T. Jaccaci, 2008.
America Awake: A Declaration of Interdependence. (New Gloucester, Maine: Unity Scholars).

Jones, Michael, 1995.
Creating an Imaginative Life. (Berkeley, California: Conari Press).

Jordan, William George, 1989.
Quoted in Stephen R. Covey, *The 7 Habits of Highly Effective People: Powerful Lessons in Personal Change.* (New York: Simon & Schuster).

Jourard, Sidney M., 1971.
The Transparent Self. (New York: D. Van Nostrand Company).

Jung, Carl G., 1970.
"The Spiritual Problem of Modern Man." In Joseph K. Davis (ed.), *Man in Crisis: Perspectives on the Individual and His World.* (Glenview, Illinois: Scott, Foresman and Company), pp. 278-293.

Jung, Carl G., 1991.
Quoted in Diane Dreher, *The Tao of Inner Peace.* First HarperPerennial Edition. (New York: HarperPerennial).

Jung, Carl G., 1994.
Quoted in Thomas Moore, *Care of the Soul: A Guide for Cultivating Depth and Sacredness in Everyday Life.* First HarperPerennial Edition. (New York: HarperCollins Publishers).

Jung, Carl G., 1996.
Quoted in James Hillman, *The Soul's Code: In Search of Character and Calling.* (New York: Random House, Inc.).

Jung, Carl G., 1998.
Quoted in Sarah Ban Breathnach, *Something More: Excavating Your Authentic Self.* (New York: Warner Books, Inc.).

Kasl, Charlotte Davis, 1994.
Finding Joy: 101 Ways to Free Your Spirit and Dance with Life. (New York: HarperPerennial).

Keen, Sam, 1997.
Praise for Gregg Levoy, *Callings: Finding and Following an Authentic Life.* (New York: Harmony Books).

Kessler, Regina, 1991.
Who Says Retirement has to be Boring? (New York: Pharos Books).

Kierkegaard, Søren, 1961.
Quoted in Carl R. Rogers, *On Becoming a Person: A Therapist's View of Psychotherapy.* (Boston, Massachusetts: Houghton Mifflin Company).

Kipling, Rudyard, 1952.
"Working Tools." In Brewster Chiselin (ed.), *The Creative Process.* (California: The Regents of the University of California), pp. 157-159.

Kiros, Tedros, 1992.
Moral Philosophy and Development: The Human Condition in Africa. Ohio University Monographs in International Studies, African Series, No. 61. (Athens, Ohio: Ohio University Press).

Klee, Paul, 1989.
Quoted in Doris J. Shallcross and Dorothy A. Sisk, *Intuition: An Inner Way of Knowing.* (Buffalo, New York: Bearly Limited).

Klopp, Hap with Brian Tarcy, 1991.
The Adventure of Leadership: An Unorthodox Business Guide from the Man Who Conquered the "North Face." (Stamford, Connecticut: Longmeadow Press).

Koestler, Arthur, 1975.
The Act of Creation. Picador Edition. (London: Pan Books Ltd.).

Krishnamurti, Jiddu, 1964.
Think on These Things. (New York: Harper & Row).

Krishnamurti, Jiddu., 1980.
Quoted in Michael Fox, *One Earth, One Mind: Personal Notes, Toward a New Natural Consciousness.* (New York: Coward, McCann, and Geoghegan).

Kristina, 2009.
http://daemonpage/introduction.php.

Kushner, Harold, 1987.
When All You've Ever Wanted Isn't Enough. First Pocket Book Printing. (New York: Pocket Books).

Land, George and Beth Jarman, 1993.
Breakpoint and Beyond: Mastering the Future – Today. First Paperback Edition. (New York: HarperCollins Publishers, Inc.).

Lane, Howard L., 1991.

On Educating Human Beings. (Chicago: Foollett Publishing Company, 1964). Quoted in Mary B. Lane, "Conflict as Viewed by Children." In James D. Quisenberry, E. Anne Eddowes, and Sandra L. Robinson (eds.), *Readings from Childhood Education,* Volume II. (Wheaton, Maryland: Association for Childhood Education International), pp. 72-75.

Laotsu, 1967.

Quoted in Clark Moustakas, *Creativity and Conformity.* (New York: D. Van Nostrand Company).

Laszlo, Ervin, 1972.

The Systems View of the World: The Natural Philosophy of the New Developments in the Sciences. (New York: George Braziller, Inc.).

Le Guin, Ursula K., 1998.

Quotted in Sarah Ban Breathnach, *Something More: Excavating Your Authentic Self.* (New York: Warner Books, Inc.).

Lee, Ilchi, 2005.

Human Technology: A Toolkit for Authentic Living. (Sedona, Arizona: Healing Society).

Leider, Richard J., 1997.

The Power of Purpose: Creating Meaning in Your Life and Work. (San Francisco: Berrett-Koehler Publishers, Inc.).

Leider, Richard J., and David A Shapiro, 1997.

Repacking Your Bags: Lighten Your Load for the Rest of Your Life. Book description. In Richard J. Leider, *The Power of Purpose: Creating Meaning in Your Life and Work.* (San Francisco: Berrett-Koehler Publishers, Inc.).

Loeb, Paul Rogat, 1999.

Soul of a Citizen: Living with Conviction in a Cynical Time. (New York: St. Martin's Griffin).

Levoy, Gregg, 1997.

Callings: Finding and Following an Authentic Life. (New York: Harmony Books).

Lombardo, Thomas and Jonathan Richter, 2004.
"Evolving Future Consciousness Through the Pursuit of Virtue." In Howard F. Didsbury Jr. and the Staff of the World Future Society (eds.), *Thinking Creatively in Turbulent Times.* (Bethesda, Maryland: World Future Society), pp. 257-288.

Long, Barry, 2003.
(Book Announcement.) In *What is Enlightenment? Wake Up to a New World,* Spring/Summer, p. 117.

Lorenz, Konrad, 1984.
Quoted in Viktor Frankl, *Man's search for Meaning: An Introduction to Logotherapy.* (New York: Simon & Schuster).

MacAllister, Jack, 1987.
Quoted in Robert Waterman, Jr., *The Renewal Factor: How the Best Get and Keep the Competitive Edge.* (Toronto: Bantam Books).

Maccoby, Michael, 1990.
Why Work: Leading the New Generation. (New York: Simon and Schuster, 1988). Quoted in Willis Harman and John Hormann, *Creative Work: The Constructive Role of Business in a Transforming Society. (*Indianapolis, Indiana: Knowledge Systems, Inc.).

Macy, Joanna, 1994.
Quoted in Matthew Fox, *The Reinvention of Work: A New Vision of Livelihood for Our Time.* (New York: HarperCollins Publishers).

Maharishi Mahesh Yogi, 1974.
Quoted in Jack Forem, *Transcendental Meditation: Maharishi Mahesh Yogi and the Science of Creative Intelligence.* (New York: E. P. Dutton & Co., Inc.).

Mailer, Norman, 1970.
"The White Negro." In Joseph K. Davis (ed.), *Man in Crisis: Perspectives on the Individual and His World.* (Glenview, Illinois: Scott, Foresman and Company), pp. 381-397.

Mandel, Terry, 1993.
"Giving Values a Voice: Marketing in the New Paradigm." In Michael Ray and Alan Rinzler (eds.), *The New Paradigm in Business: Emerging Strategies for Leadership and Organizational Change.* (New York: Jeremy P. Tarcher), pp. 164-170.

Mandela, Nelson, 1994.
Inaugural Address.

Mapes, James, J., 2003.
Quantum Leap Thinking: An Owner's Guide to the Mind. (Naperville, Illinois: Sourcebooks Incorporated).

Martin, Howard, 2000.
"Introduction." In Doc Childre and Howard Martin, *The Heartmath Solution.* First HarparCollins Paperback Edition. (New York: HarperCollins Publishers, Inc.), pp. xiv-xviii.

Maskin, Meyer, 1960.
"The Science of Personality." In Lyman Bryson (ed.), *An Outline of Man's Knowledge of the Modern World.* (New York: Nelson Doubleday, Inc.), pp. 90-117.

Maslow, Abraham H., 1962.
Toward a Psychology of Being. (Princeton, New Jersey: Nostrand).

Maslow, Abraham H., 1968.
Toward a Psychology of Being. (Princeton, New Jersey: Nostrand).

Maslow, Abraham H., 1971.
The Farther Reaches of Human Nature. (New York: Viking Press).

May, Rollo, 1969.
Love and Will. (New York: Dell Publishing Company, Inc.).

May, Rollo, 1976.
The Courage to Create. Bantam Edition. (New York: W. W. Norton and Company, Inc.).

May, Rollo, 2005.
Quoted in Vinita Hampton Wright, *The Soul Tells a Story: Engaging Creativity with Spirituality in the Writing Life.* (Downers Grove, Illinois: InterVarsity Press).

Mayor, Federico, 1994.
Quoted in Ervin Laszlo, *The Choice: Evolution or Extinction? A Thinking Person's Guide to Global Issues.* (New York: G. P. Putnam's Sons).

McConnell, Theodore A., 1971.
The Shattered Self: The Psychological and Religious Search for Selfhood. (Philadelphia: Pilgrim Press).

McDowell, Breanne Lea, 2005.
"Seeking the Authentic Self: The Impact of Nature vs. Contemporary Technocratic Society Communicated through Artistic and Written Expression."
http://www.naz.edu/dept/creativearts_therapy/docs/theses/mcdowell.pdf
.

McLuhan, Marshall (Attributed), 1970.
Quoted in Philo T. Pritzkau, *On Education for the Authentic.* (Scranton, Pennsylvania: International Textbook Company).

Mead, Margaret, 1991.
"Uniqueness and Universality." In James D. Quisenberry, E. Anne Eddowes, and Sandra L. Robinson (eds.), *Readings from Childhood Education,* Volume II. (Wheaton, Maryland: Association for Childhood Education International), pp. 320-325.

Merton, Thomas, 1961.
New Seeds of Compassion. (Norfolk, Connecticut: New Directions).

Mettler, Gordon, 1974.
Work Unlimited: A Way Out. (New York: Vantage Press).

Millikan, Robert A., 1974.
Quoted in Jack Forem, *Transcendental Meditation: Maharishi Mahesh Yogi and the Science of Creative Intelligence.* (New York: E. P. Dutton & Co., Inc.).

Montagu, Ashley, 1962.
The Humanization of Man: Our Changing Conception of Human Nature. (New York: Grove Press, Inc.).

Moore, Thomas, 1994.
Care of the Soul: A Guide for Cultivating Depth and Sacredness in Everyday Life. First HarperPerennial Edition. (New York: HarperCollins Publishers).

Moore, Thomas, 1996.
The Re-Enchantment of Everyday Life. (New York: HarperCollins Publishers).

Moore, Thomas, 1998.
Quoted in Michael Toms and Justine Willis Toms, *True Work.* (New York: Bell Tower).

Morse, Jennifer Roback, 1997.
"Who is Rational Economic Man?" *Social Philosophy & Policy,* 14(1), Winter, pp. 179 - 206.

Moss, Richard, 1998.
Words That Shine Both Ways. (Oakhurst, California: Enneas Publications).

Moustakas, Clark, 1967.
Creativity and Conformity. (New York: D. Van Nostrand Company).

Mundale, Walter F., 1997.
Praise for Richard J. Leider, *The Power of Purpose: Creating Meaning in Your Life and Work.* (San Francisco: Berrett-Koehler Publishers, Inc.).

Murphy, Joseph, 1963.
The Power of Your Subconscious Mind. (Englewood Cliffs, New Jersey: Prentice Hall, Inc.).

Murphy, Michael, 1989.
Quoted in Doris J. Shallcross and Dorothy A. Sisk, *Intuition: An Inner Way of Knowing.* (Buffalo, New York: Bearly Limited).

Murray, Henry A., 1951.
"Some Basic Psychological Assumptions and Conceptions," *Dialectica,* 5, pp. 266-292.

Neck, Christopher P., 1995.
Medicine for the Mind: Healing Words to Help You Soar. (New York: McGraw-Hill, Inc.).

Nelson, Ruben, 2000.
Quoted in Paul H. Ray and Sherry Ruth Anderson, *The Cultural Creatives: How 50 Million People Are Changing the World.* (New York: Harmony Books).

New Dimensions Media, 2008.
Broadcast, National Public Radio. November 2.

Newell, Lloyd D., 2008.
"Keep Going." *Music and the Spoken Word.* Radio Broadcast. July 27. http://www.musicandthespokenword.com/messages.

Newell, Lloyd D., 2011.
Music and the Spoken Word. Radio Broadcast. July 27. http://www.musicandthespokenword.com/messages.

Nirenberg, John, 1993.
The Living Organization: Transforming Teams into workplace Communities. (Homewood, Illinois: Business One Irwin).

Norman, Ernest L., 1960.
Cosmic Continuum. (El Cajon, California: UNARIUS, Science of Life).

Noüy, Lecomte du, 1947.
Human Destiny. (New York: Longmans, Green and Co.).

Novak, Michael, 1971.
The Experience of Nothingness. (New York: Harper & Row, Publishers).

O'Connor, Elizabeth, 1971.
Eighth Day of Creation: Discovering Your Gifts. (Washington, DC: The Servant Leadership School).

Orr, David W., 2004.
Earth in Mind: On Education, Environment, and the Human Prospect. Tenth Anniversary Edition. (Washington, DC: Island Press).

Paine, Thomas, 2000.
Quoted in Doc Childre and Howard Martin, *The Heartmath Solution.* First HarperCollins Paperback Edition. (New York: HarperCollins Publishers, Inc., 2000).

Parnes, Sidney J., 1992.
Visionizing: State-of-the-Art Processes for Encountering Innovative Excellence. (Buffalo, New York: Creative Education Foundation Press).

Parnes, Sidney J., 1997.
Optimize: The Magic of Your Mind. (Buffalo, New York: Bearly Limited).

Parnes, Sidney J. and Harold F. Harding, 1962.
"Preface." In Sidney J. Parnes and Harold F. Harding, (eds.), *A Source Book for Creative Thinking.* (New York: Charles Scribner's Sons, 1962).

Paulson, Pat A., Sharon C. Brown, and Jo Ann Wolf, 1988.
Living on Purpose. (New York: Simon & Schuster, Inc.).

Peck, M. Scott, 1993.
A World Waiting to be Born: Civility Rediscovered. (New York: Bantam Books).

Peck, M. Scott, 1995.
Quoted in Denis Waitley, *Empires of the Mind: Lessons to Lead and Succeed in a Knowledge-Based World.* (New York: William Morrow and Company, Inc.).

Peck, M. Scott, 1997.
The Road Less Traveled and Beyond: Spiritual Growth in the Age of Anxiety. (New York: Simon & Schuster).

Pearson, Carol S., 1991.
Awakening the Heroes Within: Twelve Archetypes to Help Us Find Ourselves and Transform Our World. (San Francisco: HarperCollins).

Petacchi, Donald, 1980.
Work for Being in the Machine Age. (New York: Philosophical Library).

Peterson, Severin, 1971.
A Catalog of the Ways People Grow. (New York: Ballantine Books, Inc.).

Pinchot III, Gifford and Elizabeth Pinchot, 1993.
The End of Bureaucracy and the Rise of the Intelligent Organization. (San Francisco, California: Berrett-Koehler Publishers).

Pohle, Nancy C. and Ellen L. Selover, 1999.
Awakening the Real You: Awareness through Dreams and Intuition. (Virginia Beach, Virginia: ARE Press).

Polanyi, Michael, 1990.
Quoted in John Briggs, *Fire in the Crucible: The Self-Creation of Creativity and Genius.* (Los Angeles: Jeremy P. Tarcher, Inc.).

Pologe, Bennett, 2011.
"What's a Personality? What Makes Me, Me?" http://www.aboutpsychotherapy.com/Tpersonality.htm.

Ponsoye, Pierre, 1957.
Quoted in Paul Tournier, *The Meaning of Persons.* (New York: Harper and Row, Publishers).

Powell, John, 1976.
Fully Human, Fully Alive: A New Life Through a New Vision. (Niles, Illinois: Argus Communications).

Pritzkau, Philo T., 1970.
On Education for the Authentic. (Scranton, Pennsylvania: International Textbook Company).

Quinn, Robert E., 1996.
Deep Change: Discovering the Leader Within. (San Francisco: Jossey-Brass).

Ray, Michael, 1993.
Quoted in George Land and Beth Jarman, *Breakpoint and Beyond: Mastering the Future – Today.* First Paperback Edition. (New York: HarperCollins Publishers, Inc.).

Ray, Michael, and Rochelle Myers, 1989.
Creativity in Business. (New York: Doubleday and Company, Inc.).

Ray, Paul H. and Sherry Ruth Anderson, 2000.
The Cultural Creatives: How 50 Million People Are Changing the World. (New York: Harmony Books).

Reich, Charles A., 1973.
The Greening of America. (New York: Random House).

Renesch, John, 1992.
"Preface." In John Renesch (ed.), *New Traditions in Business: Spirit and Leadership in the 21st Century.* (San Francisco: Berret-Koehler Publishers), pp. ix-xiv.

Richardson, Robert L. K., 1991.
"Wisdom-Based Junior High School Teaching." In James D. Quisenberry, E. Anne Eddowes, and Sandra L. Robinson (eds.), *Readings from Childhood Education,* Volume II. (Wheaton, Maryland: Association for Childhood Education International), pp. 102-106.

Richmond, Lewis, 1999.
Work as a Spiritual Practice: A Practical Buddhist Approach to Inner Growth and Satisfaction on the Job. (New York: Broadway Books).

Riles, Wilson, 1991.
"Bridging Cultures and Peoples." In James D. Quisenberry, E. Anne Eddowes, and Sandra L. Robinson (eds.), *Readings from Childhood Education,* Volume II. (Wheaton, Maryland: Association for Childhood Education International), pp. 171-174.

Robinson, Jonathan, 1998.
Quoted in Michael Toms and Justine Willis Toms, *True Work.* (New York: Bell Tower).

Rogers, Carl R., 1961.
On Becoming a Person: A Therapist's View of Psychotherapy. (Boston, Massachusetts: Houghton Mifflin Company).

Rogers, Carl R., 1969.
Freedom to Learn. (Columbus, Ohio: Charles Merrilll Publishing Company).

Rogers, Carl R., 1978.
Carl Rogers on Personal Power. (London: Constable).

Rogers, Carl R., 1979.
Quoted in James L Adams, *Conceptual Blockbusting: A guide to Better Ideas.* Second Edition. (New York: W. W. Norton Company).

Rolland, Romaine, 1993.
Letter to Sigmund Freud. Quoted in Daniel Goleman, "Tibetan and Western Models of Mental Health." In Daniel Goleman and Robert A. F. Thurman (eds.), *Mind Science: An East-West Dialogue.* Second Printing. (Boston, Massachusetts: Wisdom Publications), pp. 89-102.

Ross, Nancy Wilson,
Buddhism: A Way of Life and Thought. First Vintage Books Edition. (New York: Vintage Books, 1981).

Roszak, Theodore, 1975.
"Introduction." In E. F. Schumacher, *Small is Beautiful: Economics as if People Mattered.* First Perennial Library Edition. (New York: Harper & Row, Publishers, Inc., 1975), pp. 1 - 9.

Rousseau, Jean-Jacques, 2000.
Confessions. Quoted in John Colapinto, *As Nature Made Him.* (New York: HarperCollins Publishers).

Russell, Bertrand 1955.
Human Society in Ethics and Politics. (New York: Simon and Schuster).

Ryan, M. J., 2009.
"Change is Not the Enemy, Fear Is." Radio Interview. *New Dimensions Media.* Program Number 3316. November 8.

Sale, Kilpatrick, 1980.
Human Scale. (New York: Coward, McCann and Georghegan).

Satin, Mark, 1991.
Quoted in Diane Dreher, *The Tao of Inner Peace.* First HarperPerennial Edition. (New York: HarperPerennial).

Schaef, Anne Wilson, 1992.
Beyond Therapy, Beyond Science: A New Model for Healing the Whole Person. (New York: HarperCollins Publishers).

Schaeffer, Franky, 1981.
Addicted to Mediocrity: 20th Century Christians and the Arts. (Westchester, Illinois: Crossway Books).

Schlesinger, Arthur, Jr., 1960.
"The Challenge to Liberalism." In Lyman Bryson (ed.), *An Outline of Man's Knowledge of the Modern World.* (New York: Nelson Doubleday, Inc.), pp. 465-483.

Schrödinger, Erwin, 2012.
http://www.goodreads.com/quotes/tag/perception.

Schubert, William H., 1993.
"Curriculum Reform." In Gordon Cawelti (ed.), *Challenges and Achievements of American Education.* (Alexandria, Virginia: Association for Supervision and Curriculum Development), pp. 80-115.

Schuller, Robert H., 1975.
Move Ahead with Possibility Thinking. (Old Tappan, New Jersey: Pillar Books).

Schumacher, E. F., 1975.
Small is Beautiful: Economics as if People Mattered. First Perennial Library Edition. (New York: Harper & Row, Publishers, Inc.).

Schumacher, E. F., 1994.
Quoted in Matthew Fox, *The Reinvention of Work: A New Vision of Livelihood for Our Time.* (New York: HarperCollins Publishers).

Schweitzer, Albert, 1955.
The Philosophy of Civilization. (New York: The Macmillan Company). Quoted in Erich Fromm, *The Sane Society.* (New York: Fawcett World Library).

Schweitzer, Albert, 2004.
Quoted in Vance Secretan, *Inspire: What Great Leaders Do.* (Hoboken, New Jersey: John Wiley & Sons, Inc.).

Scott-Bader Commonwealth, 1990.
"Preamble to the Constitution of the Commonwealth." Quoted in Willis Harman and John Hormann, *Creative Work: The Constructive Role of Business in a Transforming Society.*(Indianapolis, Indiana: Knowledge Systems, Inc.).

Secretan, Vance, 2004.
Inspire: What Great Leaders Do. (Hoboken, New Jersey: John Wiley & Sons, Inc.).

Seifert, Harvey, 1968.
Power Where the Action Is. (Philadelphia: The Westminster Press).

Sejnowski, Tery, 1998.
Quoted in Michael S. Gazzaniga, *The Mind's Past.* (Berkeley: University of California Press).

Senge, Peter, 2003.
"The Challenge of Our Moment: A Roundtable Discussion with Don Beck, Brian Swimme, and Peter Senge," *What is Enlightenment? Wake Up to a New World,* Spring/Summer, pp. 42-54.

Senge, Peter M., 1995.
Praise for Michael Jones, *Creating an Imaginative Life.* (Berkley, California: Conari Press).

Shallcross, Doris J. and Dorothy A. Sisk, 1989.
Intuition: An Inner Way of Knowing. (Buffalo, New York: Bearly Limited).

Sheehan, George A., 1987.
Quoted in Robert Waterman Jr., *The Renewal Factor: How the Best Get and Keep the Competitive Edge.* (Toronto: Bantam Books).

Siebert, Al, 1996.
The Survivor Personality: Why Some People are Smarter, Stronger, and More Skillful at Handling Life's Difficulties ... and How You Can Be, Too. (New York: The Berkley Publishing Group).

Siebert, Al, 2005.
The Resiliency Factor: Master Change, Thrive Under Pressure, and Bounce Back from Setbacks. (San Francisco: Berrett-Koehler Publishers, Inc.).

Singer, Jerome, 1981.
"Put Your Daydreams to Work." In Reader's Digest (ed.), *Mind Power: How to Develop It ... Use It ... Expand It!* (New York: Berkley Books), pp. 175-179.

Sinnott, Edmund W., 1960.
Quoted in Harold G. Wolff, "The Mind-Body Relationship." In Lyman Bryson (ed.), *An Outline of Man's Knowledge of the Modern World.* (New York: Nelson).

Sirolli, Ernesto, 1999.
Ripples from the Zambezi. (Gabriola Island, British Columbia, Canada: New Society Publishers).

Sitwell, Edith, 1989.
Quoted in Doris J. Shallcross and Dorothy A. Sisk, *Intuition: An Inner Way of Knowing.* (Buffalo, New York: Bearly Limited).

Smith, Adam, 1991.
Quoted in Robert L. Heilbroner, *An Inquiry into the Human Prospect: Looked at Again for the 1990s.* (New York: W. W. Norton and Company, Inc.).

Snyder, Agnes, 1991.
"The Roots of Growth." In James D. Quisenberry, E. Anne Eddowes, and Sandra L. Robinson (eds.), *Readings from Childhood Education,* Volume II. (Wheaton, Maryland: Association for Childhood Education International), pp. 304-307.

Spady, Richard J. and Cecil H. Bell, Jr., 1997.
The Search for Enlightened Leadership. Volume One: Applying New Administrative Theory. (Olympia, Washington: Panpress Publishers).

Spady, Richard J. and Richard S. Kirby, 2002.
The Leadership of Civilization Building: Administrative and Civilization Theory, Symbolic Dialogue, and Citizen Skills for the 21st Century. (Seattle: Forum Foundation).

Spalding, Baird T., 1967.
Quoted Stanwood Cobb, *The Importance of Creativity.* (Metuchen, New Jersey: The Scarecrow Press, Inc.).

Spencer, Sabina, 1990.
Quoted in Stanford M. Janger and Amy Edmondson, "Business in Transformation." Afterword. In Willis Harman and John Hormann, *Creative Work: The Constructive Role of Business in a Transforming Society.*(Indianapolis, Indiana: Knowledge Systems, Inc.).

Spivey, Ted R., 1970.
Modern Civilization's Cross: The Man-Woman Relationship." In Joseph K. Davis (ed.), *Man in Crisis: Perspectives on the Individual and His World.* (Glenview, Illinois: Scott, Foresman and Company), pp. 336-348.

Stevenson, R. L., 1980.
Quoted in Michael Fox, *One Earth, One Mind: Personal Notes, Toward a New Natural Consciousness.* (New York: Coward, McCann, and Geoghegan).

Stewart, John, 2004.

Quoted in Thomas Lombardo and Jonathan Richter, "Evolving Future Consciousness Through the Pursuit of Virtue." In Howard F. Didsbury Jr. and the Staff of the World Future Society (eds.), *Thinking Creatively in Turbulent Times.* (Bethesda, Maryland: World Future Society), pp 257-288.

Stuart, Ninian, 1983.

Worldviews: Crosscultural Explorations of Human Beliefs. (New York: Charles Scribner's and Sons).

Swimme, Brian, 2003.

Personal Blurb. "The Challenge of Our Moment: A Roundtable Discussion with Don Beck, Brian Swimme, and Peter Senge," *What is Enlightenment? Wake Up to a New World,* Spring/Summer, pp. 42-54.

Swindoll, Charles R., 1983.

Growing Strong in the Seasons of Life. (Portland, Oregon: Multnomah Press).

Swindoll, Charles, R., 1995.

Living Above the Level of Mediocrity. In Charles Swindoll, *The Collected Works of Charles Swindoll.* (New York: Inspirational Press).

Talku, Tarthang, 1998.

Quoted in Michael Toms and Justine Willis Toms, *True Work.* (New York: Bell Tower).

Terkel, Studs, 1994.

Quoted in Matthew Fox, *The Reinvention of Work: A New Vision of Livelihood for Our Time.* (New York: HarperCollins Publishers).

Theobald, Robert, 1981.

Beyond Despair: A Policy Guide to the Communications Era. Revised Edition. (Cabin John, Maryland: Seven Locks Press, Inc.).

Thiss, Tom, 1995.

The Wizard of Is. (Minneapolis, Minnesota: Fairview Press).

Thurston, Mark, 1997.
Soul-Purpose: Discovering and Fulfilling Your Destiny. St. Martin's Paperbacks Edition. (New York: St. Martin's Press).

Tillich, Paul, 1952.
The Courage to Be. (New Haven, Connecticut: Yale University Press).

Todaro, Michael P., 1989.
Economic Development in the Third World. Fourth Edititon. (New York: Longman, Inc.).

Toms, Michael and Justine Willis Toms, 1998.
True Work. (New York: Bell Tower).

Torrance, E. Paul, 1979.
The Search for Satori and Creativity. (Buffalo, New York: Creative Education Foundation).

Tournier, Paul, 1957.
The Meaning of Persons. (New York: Harper and Row, Publishers).

Toynbee, A. J., 1958.
Quoted in *The Reader's Digest,* October. In Robert Andrews (ed.), *The Columbia Dictionary of Quotations.* (New York: Columbia University Press).

Toynbee, A. J., 1976.
Quoted in Silvano Arieti, *Creativity: The Magic Synthesis.* (New York: Basic Books, Inc.).

Tulku, Tarthang, 1989.
Quoted in Michael Ray and Rochelle Myers, *Creativity in Business.* (New York: Doubleday and Company, Inc.).

Universal House of Justice, 1985.
"The Promise of World Peace." Statement to the Peoples of the World. (Bahá'í World Center, Haifa, Israel), October.

Utne, Eric, 1997.
(Book Endorsement.) Richard J. Leider, *The Power of Purpose: Creating Meaning in Your Life and Work.* (San Francisco: Berrett-Koehler Publishers, Inc.).

Vaclav, Havel, 1993.
Quoted in Michael Ray and Alan Rinzler, "Social and Environmental Responsibility." In Michael Ray and Alan Rinzler (eds.), *The New Paradigm in Business: Emerging Strategies for Leadership and Organizational Change.* (New York: Jeremy P. Tarcher), pp. 185 - 189.

Viscott, David, 1984.
The Viscott Method. (New York: Pocket Books).

Waitley, Denis, 1995.
Empires of the Mind: Lessons to Lead and Succeed in a Knowledge-Based World. (New York: William Morrow and Company, Inc.).

Walsch, Neale Donald, 2005.
"Foreword." In Ilchi Lee, Human *Technology: A Toolkit for Authentic Living.* (Sedona, Arizona: Healing Society); pp. 9-10.

Weaver, Henry Grady, 1965.
The Mainspring of Human Progress. 7th Printing. (New York: Foundation for Economic Education, Inc.).

Weiss, Frederick A., 1970.
"Self-Alienation: Dynamics and Therapy." In Joseph K. Davis (ed.), *Man in Crisis: Perspectives on the Individual and His World.* (Glenview, Illinois: Scott, Foresman and Company), 294-306.

Welk, Lawrence, 1968.
Guidelines for Successful Living. (New York: The New American Library, Inc.).

Wenger, Win, 1992.
Creating Wealth for Yourself and Others in Countries Without Capital: Techniques for Solving Problems, for Creativity, and for Innovation. (Unpublished Manuscript). (Project Renaissance, Gaitthersburg, Maryland).

Wenger, Win, 2004.
"Visiting the Future: March 27, 2472," *Winsights,* 76, May/June. http://www.winwnger.com/part76.htm.

White, Jennifer, 2001.
Drive Your People Wild Without Driving Them Crazy: Leadership Lessons for a Chaotic World. (Oxford, U.K.: Capstone Publishing Ltd).

Whitehead, Alfred North, 1959.
Adventures of Ideas: A Brilliant History of Mankind's Great Thoughts. Third Printing. (New York: Mentor Books).

Wilson, Thomasyne Lightfoote, 1991.
"Let's Join Hands for Human Understanding." In James D. Quisenberry, E. Anne Eddowes, and Sandra L. Robinson (eds.), *Readings from Childhood Education,* Volume II. (Wheaton, Maryland: Association for Childhood Education International), pp. 183-192.

Wolff, Harold G., 1960.
"The Mind-Body Relationship." In Lyman Bryson (ed.), *An Outline of Man's Knowledge of the Modern World.* (New York: Nelson Doubleday, Inc.), pp. 41 – 72.

Wolf, Naomi, 1997.
Quoted in Lorne A. Adrian, *The Most Important Thing I Know.* (New York: MJF Books).

Wolf, Susan, 1997.
"Happiness and Meaning: Two Aspects of the Good Life," *Social Philosophy and Policy,* 14(1), Winter, pp. 207 - 225.

Wright, Vinita Hampton, 2005.
The Soul Tells a Story: Engaging Creativity with Spirituality in the Writing Life. (Downers Grove, Illinois: InterVarsity Press).

Young, Isobel Imrie G., 1982.
There Will Never Be Another You. (Commonwealth Press).

Yunus, Muhammad with Karl Weber, 2010.
Building Social Business: The New Kind of Capitalism that Serves Humanity's Most Pressing Needs. (New York: Public Affairs).

Zinsser, William, 1992.
"College Pressures" In The HarperCollins Editors (eds.), *The Writer's Library: Education.* (New York: HarperCollins College Publishers), pp. 57-65.

Zukav, Gary, 1990.
The Seat of the Soul. First Fireside Edition. (New York: Simon & Schuster).

Zukav, Gary, 1993.
"Evolution and Business." In Michael Ray and Alan Rinzler (eds.), *The New Paradigm in Business: Emerging Strategies for Leadership and Organizational Change.* (New York: Jeremy P. Tarcher), pp. 239 - 249.

CPSIA information can be obtained at www.ICGtesting.com
Printed in the USA
LVOW13s1744150414

381822LV00004B/726/P

9 781622 875153